"Restaurant patrons looking for quality dining have Zagat to guide their cuisine needs. For the recruitment industry, the name is Weddle … Peter Weddle that is."

American Staffing Association

Also by Peter Weddle

The Success Matrix: How to Find a Great Job & Hang Onto It

The Career Activist Republic

Work Strong: Your Personal Career Fitness System

Recognizing Richard Rabbit: A Fable About Being True to Yourself

Career Fitness: How to Find, Win & Keep the Job You Want in the 1990's

WEDDLE's Guide to Employment Sites on the Internet

WEDDLE's Guide to Association Web Sites

WEDDLE's Guide to Staffing Firms & Employment Agencies

Internet Resumes: Take the Net to Your Next Job

CliffsNotes: Finding a Job on the Web

CliffsNotes: Writing a Great Resume

WEDDLE's WIZNotes: Fast Facts on Job Boards
>   Human Resource Professionals
>   Engineering Professionals
>   Sales & Marketing Professionals
>   Finance & Accounting Professionals
>   Scientists
>   Managers & Executives
>   Women Professionals
>   Recent College Graduates

'Tis of Thee: A Son's Search for the Meaning of Patriotism

Walden 4G: A Novel About Rediscovering Hopefulness (and America's Secret Utopia) due in the spring of 2012

What People are Saying about WEDDLE's Books & Services

"A wealth of useful, updated information."

Library Journal

"This book is a great resource. ... It's like a travel guide to job boards."

Corporate Recruiter

"Highly recommended!"

Richard Nelson Bolles, author of What Color is Your Parachute?

"When in doubt, consult WEDDLE's ... an industry standard."

HRWIRE

"The WEDDLE's Guide to Employment Web Sites supplies clear, completely current information about each site's services, features and fees—helping users instantly determine which site best meets their needs."

ExecuNet, The Center for Executive Careers

"I found your book in the public library. Recently, I purchased my own copy from Amazon.com. It is a terrific book for breaking down the complexity of looking for a job. Thank you for writing this book."

Job Seeker

"...an incredibly useful tool in helping individuals focus their job search on the Web."

Career Counselor

JOB NATION

The 100 Best Employment Sites on the Web

Peter Weddle

ISBN: 978-1-928734-69-7

The information that appears in this Guide was obtained directly from the Web-sites themselves. Most of the data provided in the Site Profiles were collected in early 2011. Each site completed an extensive questionnaire about its services, features and fees and then certified the accuracy of its responses. The Internet changes quickly, however, and we work continuously to keep our information current. If you find a discrepancy in a site's profile, please notify WEDDLE's by telephone at 203.964.1888 or on the Internet at corporate@weddles.com.

Special thanks to the WEDDLE's research and production team, including Meagan Micozzi, Christina Levere and our two vice presidents of security, Paddy and Luca.

Special discounts on bulk quantities of WEDDLE's books are available for libraries, corporations, professional associations and other organizations. For details, please contact WEDDLE's at 203.964.1888.

WEDDLE's
www.weddles.com
2052 Shippan Avenue
Stamford, CT 06902

Where People Matter Most

Contents

What Are Employment Sites?

An employment site is an Internet-site specifically designed to help people who are looking for a new or better job connect with employers and staffing firm recruiters who are looking to fill open positions.

These sites can be:

Job Boards

Job boards typically publish employment ads on the Internet as well as information and support for successful job search. Most job boards offer their visitors some or all of the following: a searchable database of employment opportunities and often, a database where job seekers can post their resume or profile, plus tips on resume writing, interviewing and other topics related to finding a new or better job.

Career Portals

Career portals typically provide all of the services of a job board as well as information and support for individual career management. In addition to a job and, possibly, a resume/profile database, a career portal will provide tools for such tasks as selecting a career field, setting career goals, dealing with career roadblocks and problems, and determining the direction and content of a person's professional development.

Social Media Sites

Social media sites help people network online for both job search and career advancement. As their name indicates, most social media sites have a decidedly social purpose, but they can also be used to expand a person's range of professional or occupational contacts and increase their visibility among their peers and prospective employers. In addition, a growing number of social media sites now also post employment opportunities either in a separate database or on pages devoted to specific employers.

A Summary of Services Offered by Employment Sites

For Those Seeking a New or Better Job

> Access to employment opportunities in the job seeker's home town and around the world.

> Private, automated notification of job openings that match their employment objective.

> Information about effective job search techniques on the Internet and off.

> Resources for a successful job search, such as resume writing assistance and interviewing guides.

> Links to additional job search resources located at other sites.

For Those Seeking to Advance Their Career

> Skills for effective career self-management.

> Resources for career success (e.g., assessment tests, peer-to-peer discussion forums).

> Skills training and certification in individual career fields and select topics.

> Links to additional career management resources located at other sites.

> Information and resources for a better work-life balance.

Do Employment Sites Work?

In today's demanding job market, there's no room for wasted time and effort. It's perfectly appropriate, therefore, to ask should you even bother to use online employment sites.

Pundits, of course, will have their opinion of what constitutes the correct answer to that question. We at WEDDLE's, however, believe that it's the actual users of job boards, career portals and social media sites – the job seekers, employers and recruiters who rely on their services – who know best. So, we've asked them.

WEDDLE's (www.weddles.com) is a research and publishing company specializing in employment. Every year since 1999, we've conducted an online survey of the behaviors and beliefs of job seekers, employers and staffing firm recruiters. It is one of the longest running studies of the job market in the United States. What follows is a summary of the most recent results of the survey, which were tabulated in 2011.

The Job Seeker's Perspective

The survey first sought to pinpoint what was working best for job seekers. It asked them, "How did you find your last job?" The top five responses were:

> Answered an ad posted on an Internet job board – 31.1 percent

> Sent a resume into the company – 9.8 percent

> Got a tip from a friend – 8.2 percent

> Answered an ad posted on a company's Web-site – 6.6 percent (tie)

> Answered an ad in a newspaper – 6.6 percent (tie).

If the votes cast for posting a resume on a job board were added to those cast for responding to an ad posted there, the total for job boards rises to almost one-in-four (37.7 percent) of the responses.

Even more impressive, when asked "How do you expect to find your next job?", almost half of the respondents (45.8 percent) cited either responding to an ad or posting their resume on a job board.

That finding was more than four times greater than the #2 response which was "Sending a resume into the company" at 11.9 percent and better than five times greater than the #3 response which was "Getting a call from a headhunter" at 8.5 percent.

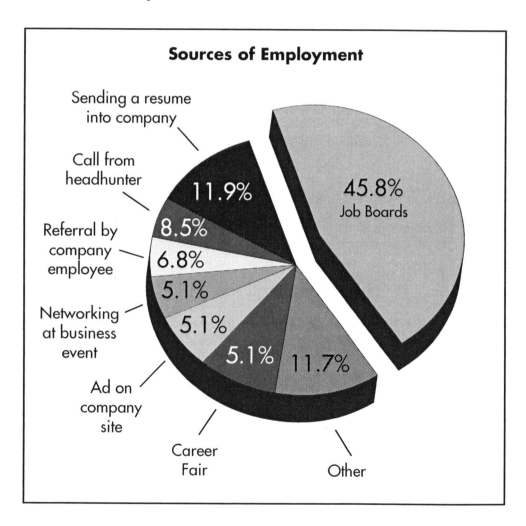

Job seekers also spend a lot of time on employer's own Web-sites, so the survey asked "How helpful are the career areas on employer Web-sites?." The single largest response – garnering exactly half the votes – was "Moderately helpful." That was followed by "Very helpful" at 18.9 percent and "Not help-ful – not enough information about the employer's open positions" at 17.2 percent.

Social media sites have also attracted a lot of attention from job seekers, so the survey asked "Have you used a social media site (e.g., Facebook, Linked-In) in your job search?." The results suggest that, despite their social popular-ity, these platforms are still in the very early stages of adoption for job search. The two responses with the greatest support were "Yes, but just a little" and "No, but I intend to in the near future," both of which garnered 29.3 percent of the votes. The next highest response was "No, and I never will" which cap-tured 24.1 percent of the ballots.

As a follow up, the survey asked those who had used social media sites to rate their effectiveness in job search. The largest response was "Somewhat helpful" which captured 36.6 percent of the ballots. In second place was "No more helpful than other job search techniques," which was cited by 29.3 percent of the respondents.

About the Respondents

Typically, WEDDLE's job seeker surveys attract 3-5,000 unique respondents each year. They are a diverse group with a relatively wide range of back-grounds and experience. For these particular results, they were 55 percent female, 45 percent male. Over a quarter (28.9 percent) were older than 56 years of age and exactly a quarter were 31-40 years old.

The largest group (41.1 percent) described themselves as "Currently em-ployed, but actively looking for another job," followed by "Not currently em-ployed and actively seeking a job" at 30.4 percent and "Currently employed, but thinking about making a job change this year" at 21.4 percent.

Of those who were in the job market or intend to be, most were mid-level professionals (32.8 percent), followed by senior level professionals (13.8 percent) and entry-level professionals (12.1 percent). Both the administra-tion and skilled trades categories also received votes with each receiving 6.9 percent of the ballots cast.

The Employer's & Staffing Firm Recruiter's Perspective

The survey first explored where recruiters were focusing their recruiting efforts. Or, to put it another way, "Which sourcing strategy provides the best quality applicants?."

The largest single response, cited by better than four-out-of-ten of the survey respondents (40.7 percent) was "Posting jobs on a commercial job board." The rest of the top five responses and the percentage of respondents that cited them were as follows:

> Their employee referral program – 12.9 percent

> Posting jobs on their own Web-site – 11.1 percent

> Using social networking sites – 9.3 percent

> Using a staffing firm – 5.6 percent (tie)

> Advertising jobs in newspapers – 5.6 percent (tie).

The survey also asked "What percentage of your total openings are posted online?." More than three-quarters of the respondents (77.3 percent) said that they were now posting over half of their vacancies online. More than a third (34.8 percent) were actually posting 91 percent or more. And, just 6.1 percent weren't using the Internet at all.

Was that strategy working?

Over half of the respondents (50.8 percent) reported that they are now hiring over half of their new employees online. And, an astonishing 25.4 percent were hiring 91 percent or more of their new workers on the Internet. Just 11.1 percent were hiring 5 percent or fewer.

The survey also asked employers and recruiters "Of the openings posted online, where are the majority posted?." Better than four-out-of-ten (41.7 percent) posted their vacancies at one or more job boards. More than a quarter (28.3 percent) posted them at their own Web-site and one or more job boards. Fewer than one-out-of-ten (8.3 percent) posted their openings at their own Web-site and one or more social media sites. And, just 15 percent posted their openings only on their own Web-site, while even fewer (6.7 percent) posted them exclusively at one or more social media sites.

Finally, the survey probed employers and recruiters to determine how satisfied they were with the new hires they found at job boards, career portals and social media sites. The survey asked "How would you rate the caliber of your new hires sourced online?." Over half (54.2 percent) described them as either "Above average employees" or "Among our best employees." Not quite a third (31.1 percent) said they were "Average employees," and a miniscule 1.6 percent called them "A hiring mistake."

So, What's the Final Conclusion?

Employment sites on the Internet work.

They can't guarantee anyone that they'll land a job, but they can and do connect job seekers to some of the best employment opportunities in the workplace.

What's the key to optimizing your chances of success with an employment site? Use the best of those sites and use them in the best way possible. This Guide will show you how to do both.

Why Do You Need This Guide?

For most of the 20th Century, job seekers had only a very limited number of ways to find employment opportunities. Basically, they had to rely on their local newspaper and a small circle of friends and colleagues to uncover available openings. It was, at best, a hit-or-miss system that all too often failed to serve either job seekers or employers and recruiters very well.

In today's job market, exactly the opposite problem has emerged. There are now more than 100,000 job boards and career portals as well as an ever-growing number of social media sites on the Internet. They are operated by:

> commercial companies

> professional and trade associations

> newspapers and magazines

> radio and television stations

> college, university and trade school alumni organizations

> churches and church-affiliated groups

> clubs, sororities, fraternities and other affinity groups.

They offer job seekers so many choices, it's hard to know which are most likely to provide the support and assistance they need and deserve.

How Can This Guide Help?

This guide has been compiled by one of the world's leading experts in Internet employment sites. In fact, the American Staffing Association called him "the Zagat of the online employment services industry." His name is Peter Weddle.

Peter has been researching and writing about job boards, career portals and social media sites almost since they were first created. He has been a columnist for *The Wall Street Journal*, CNN.com and *National Business Employment Weekly*. He is also the founder and current CEO of the International

Association of Employment Web Sites (IAEWS), the trade organization of the global online employment services industry. Its site is located at www. EmploymentWebSites.org.

Peter has used this background and experience to determine his pick of the

100 best employment sites on the Web. Are there other exemplary sites available to job seekers, employers and staffing firm recruiters? Of course. The sites profiled here, however, represent those that Peter considers the elite of the field ... sites that have proven by their consistently high level of service, commitment to continuous improvement, and/or their innovative products and services, the very best the Internet has to offer to individuals in the job market, today and tomorrow.

What's in Job Nation?

Job Nation has been specifically designed for people who are looking for employment opportunities, including those:

> actively searching for a new or better job,

> seeking to make a career change,

> setting goals to advance their career, or

> simply exploring the job market out of curiosity.

Whether you're a first time job seeker or a mid-career professional, a senior executive or an hourly worker, whether you want a full time position or part time, contract, consulting or free agent work, *Job Nation* will help you find the right job boards, career portals and social media sites to succeed at your employment objective.

Each of the sites is described in a full-page profile. These profiles look much like the easy-to-read-and-use descriptions that appear in popular travel guides. They offer a detailed set of information carefully tailored to the needs of job seekers.

> This information includes the number and kinds of jobs that are posted on the site, the primary salary ranges and geographic locations of those jobs, whether the site has a resume or profile database, whether there is a fee to store a resume or profile in that database, whether the site takes steps to protect a person's confidentiality, and much more.

In addition, there is also a Cross Reference Index of the profiled sites that organizes them according to the career fields, industries and employment situations (e.g., free lance work) they cover. The Index is particularly important because Web-site names do not always accurately describe the full range of a site's capabilities and services.

A Detailed Description of the Information You Get

Each site profile identifies the site by its name, URL or address on the Internet, and its parent organization. Then, additional descriptive information is provided in six sections:

> **General Site Information**

> **Job Postings**

> **Resume Services**

> **Other Services**

> **Site's Self Description**

> **Contact Information**

The information that is included in each of these sections is described below.

❏ General Site Information

Date activated online:

The date the site first appeared on the Internet or World Wide Web.

Importance to you:

Although not always the case, the longer a site has been in operation, the more developed its services and reliable its performance.

Location of the site headquarters:

The city and state in the United States or the city and country where the site's parent company or organization is located.

Importance to you:

A local address adds credibility to a site's claim that it reaches employers in a specific geographic area.

Number of people who visit the site:

The number of individuals who visit the site in a given month, with each person counted just once, regardless of how many times they came to the site. This metric is called unique visitors per month.

Importance to you:

The number of people who visit a site each month is important to you for two reasons: (1) The figure will help you compare sites to determine which are the most popular among other job seekers. (2) It will also help you to evaluate the level of competition you will face from other job seekers when applying for openings posted on a given site.

Time spent on site:

The time visitors spend on a site measured in minutes per visit or in the number of pages of information that they view while there (page views per visitor).

Importance to you:

This figure is an indication of the quality of the information provided by a site. The more time visitors spend on the site or the more pages of information they view, the higher the site's perceived value.

❑ Job Postings

Post full time jobs:

Does the site post ads for full time positions?

Importance to you:

Indicates whether the site's employment opportunities will support your job search objective.

Post part time/contract/consulting jobs: Does the site post ads for part time, contract and/or consulting positions?

Importance to you: *Indicates whether the site's employment opportunities will support your job search objective.*

Most prevalent types of jobs posted: What are the predominant kinds of jobs currently being posted by recruiters?

Importance to you: *Helps you determine the strength of the site's job database in your particular career field or for your specific employment objective.*

Distribution: What is the geographic focus of the site's job postings: regional, national, international?

Importance to you: *Indicates whether the site's employment opportunities are located either where you currently live or would like to.*

In some cases, abbreviations have been used to denote the kinds of jobs currently being posted on a site. These abbreviations are presented in the Table below.

Key to Career Field Abbreviations Used in the Web-site Profiles

AD-Administrative	HR-Human Resources
CM-Computer-related	IS-Info Systems/Technology
CN-Communications	MG-Management
DP-Data Processing	OP-Operations
EC-Electronic Commerce	PG-Programming
EN-Engineering	SM-Sales/Marketing
FA-Finance/Accounting	

Number of job postings:

What is the total number of jobs posted on the site at any given point in time?

Importance to you:

Indicates the extent of the opportunity available to you at the site so that you can determine whether it would be worth your while to visit.

Top salary levels of jobs:

What salary range (or ranges) appears most frequently among the jobs posted on the site?

Importance to you:

Helps you determine whether the jobs posted on the site are at the right compensation level for you.

Source of postings:

How were the job postings on the site acquired: direct from employers, from search and staffing firms, cross-posted from other job boards, or copied from other sites.

Importance to you:

Helps you determine who will be involved in screening your credentials and the quality of an opportunity: postings from employers, search and staffing firms, and those cross-posted from other job boards are more likely to be genuine and current than those that are copied from other sites.

❏ Resume Services

Are resumes or profiles posted on-site:

Indicates whether you can store a resume or profile on the site.

Importance to you: *Some sites archive resumes and/or profiles in a database that they then make available to recruiters. The database may be completely open to the public or accessible only in part (i.e., your contact information is protected until you release it).*

How long can you store: How many days, months or years can a resume or profile be left in the site's database without re-posting or updating it?

Importance to you: *If you are actively searching for a position, indicates how frequently you must return to the site to re-post your resume; if you have found a position, indicates whether you should return to the site to delete your resume from its database.*

Who can post a resume: Is posting a resume/profile on the site restricted to special categories of users (e.g., association members, those who register with the site, those in a certain career field or in a certain industry)?

Importance to you: *Indicates whether or not you are eligible to post your resume/profile in the site's database.*

Fee to post: Must you pay a fee to store your resume or profile in the site's database?

Importance to you: *There's nothing wrong with paying a reasonable fee to post your resume on a site, but make sure you assess the value of doing so. To evaluate the fee, use* *the length of time the resume will be stored on the site and the source(s) of the site's job postings to determine how much visibility you are likely to get with the kinds of recruiters you want to reach.*

Confidentiality available: Indicates whether the site will help to protect your privacy by: (a) blocking out contact information from your resume, (b) prohibiting employer access to the resume database (in which case, the site serves as an intermediary between you and the recruiter until you decide to reveal your identity), or (c) some other feature.

Importance to you: *Those sites that protect your privacy enable you to search for a new or better job whenever and wherever you want. They ensure that you remain in charge of your job search effort and preserve your flexibility in the job market.*

❑ Other Services

Is a listserv/discussion forum offered: This feature enables site visitors to connect with their peers online and discuss professional, trade and/or business issues with them.

Importance to you: *This feature provides three important benefits: (1) you can network with a wider circle of contacts than those in your local area; (2) you can expand your knowledge and visibility in your field; and (3) you can demonstrate your expertise where recruiters can see it.*

Are assessment instruments offered:

Indicates whether there are skill, personality and other tests available on the site.

Importance to you:

The data provided by these tests can enhance your self-knowledge and ensure that you compete for a job you can do well in an organization where you will be comfortable.

Automated job agent:

A job agent is a free service that will automatically compare your specified employment objective with all of the jobs posted on the site and notify you privately whenever a match occurs.

Importance to you:

You can save time and effort by using a site's job agent. While the agent is checking openings for you on the site, you can be evaluating other opportunities or networking at other sites.

Career info provided:

Indicates whether the site offers job search and career management information (e.g., interviewing tips) as well as job postings.

Importance to you:

Helps you select those sites that are likely to be most beneficial to you. There are only so many hours in the day, so use sites that provide both appropriate job opportunities and a range of information that will help you achieve your employment objectives.

Links to other sites:

Does the site provide hypertext links or electronic connections to other sites with career and/or job search information that can be helpful to you?

Importance to you: *Helps you evaluate the potential benefit of a site to you.*

❏ Site's Self-Description

A 50-100 word description of the site's features, services and fees, written by the site. These descriptions are edited for length, grammatical correctness and clarity, as necessary.

Importance to you: *The content and tone of the site's self description will give you a feel for its understanding of your job search and career requirements as well as its commitment to customer service.*

❏ Contact Information

Provides the name, e-mail address and telephone number of the site's preferred point of contact.

A Word on Sites That Fail to Report Information

When a site fails to provide any of the information described above, that discrepancy is noted in its Profile by the term "Not Reported."

Generally speaking, those sites that are most open about their capabilities—by providing complete and detailed information about their services, features and fees—are your best bet for achieving success in your online job search.

What's the Best Way to Use Job Nation?

WEDDLE's SmartSearch™ Process provides a structured way for you to make smart decisions when selecting employment sites. It will help you find those sites that are most likely to yield the best results as you pursue your specific employment objective.

The SmartSearch™ Process

Let's face it; finding the employment sites that will work best for you is no easy task. In essence, you have two choices:

> You can follow the herd and apply for jobs posted at the same sites that everyone else is using,

or

> You can "shop" for employment sites with the same consumer savvy you use when looking for any other important service or product.

If your choice is to be a smart consumer, **WEDDLE's SmartSearch™** process is just what you need to get the job done!

The SmartSearch™ process is based on a very simple premise: You can be an expert in job search <u>and</u> in using the Internet and still fail to connect with your dream job **if** you do not look for that opportunity at the right Web-sites. Indeed, selecting the best sites for your employment objective is a prerequisite for successfully using the Internet to find a new or better job.

SmartSearch™ is a proven, 5-step, "job seeker friendly" process for making smart site selections. It draws on the experience and lessons-learned of successful online job seekers and the rich array of site information found in *Job Nation*.

Step 1: Check out the Field.

Use the Cross Reference Index to identify those employment sites that serve your occupational field, industry and/or geographic location.

To make sure you give yourself adequate access to the opportunities posted online and adequate visibility to the employers looking at resumes online, select and use at least five sites. WEDDLE's recommends the following formula:

$$2GP + 3N = 1GJ$$

where:

2GP represents two general purpose employment sites (sites that give you access to opportunities in a wide array of industries and locations).

3N represents three niche employment sites:

> one that specializes in the industry in which you want to work,

> one that specializes in your career field, and

> one that specializes in the geographic location where you live or want to.

Using that array of sites will optimize your access to opportunities and provide the best assurance you will find **1GJ**: one great job that's just right for you.

Step 2: Evaluate the Possibilities.

Use the Site Profiles in *Job Nation* and your own research to evaluate each of your site options. The profiles provide a wide range of descriptive information about each site that can be used to:

> Assess each site on its own merits

and

> Compare each site to all of your other options.

One way to perform these assessments and comparisons is to focus on a sub-set of the information provided in the Site Profiles. We think using this shorthand method as your selection criteria can help you make quick and accurate evaluations of alternative sites and speed you to those that are most likely to invigorate your job search. It seems only fitting, therefore, that the elements of the shorthand method, which are listed, should form the acronym OASIS.

We suggest that you use OASIS to narrow the number of sites you are considering down to 5-8 strong possibilities. Then, use the full Site Profiles of each to conduct a detailed evaluation of the match between its services, features and fees and the kind and level of support you want.

OASIS:

O   Opportunities for employment: the number and kinds of jobs posted on the site (e.g., full time, part time)

Do they match your employment objective?   Yes ___ No ___

A   Availability of a job agent: an email notification of openings that are right for you

Can you sign up a free job agent?   Yes ___ No ___

S   Salary ranges of the posted jobs:

Is the pay appropriate for your experience level?

Yes ___ No ___

I   Investment: the cost of services or information provided on the site

Are there any fees you must pay?   Yes ___ No ___

S   Support for job search and career management

Can you get the information or service you need?

Yes ___ No ___

Step 3: Visit the Sites Online.

The best way to assess your options further is to pay each of the 5-8 sites a visit online. Sites that seem all but identical on paper often have a very different look and feel on the Internet. The key is to find those sites that provide the best experience for you: they are easy for you to use and they provide the specific kind of information and support you want. Or, to put it another way, the best sites are those that provide the optimum return on your investment of time and effort when using them.

Step 4: Make Your Selection & Track Your Results.

Just as you would with a traditional job search campaign, the best way to look for a job online is to select and use several venues or sites simultaneously. As previously noted, WEDDLE's suggests that you use five sites – two general purpose and three niche sites – regularly. Each will provide you with a different channel into the job market, which is an important capability because it's impossible to know, in advance, which organizations will be looking where on the Web for prospective employees.

In addition, be a good consumer. Keep track of each site's performance—using such metrics as the number of jobs it posts in your field, the number of jobs it posts at your skill level and the caliber of the employers that post those jobs—and refer to those data the next time and every time you "shop" for a job board.

Step 5: Continually Reassess and Fine Tune Your Selections.

It's easy to become creatures of habit and return to the same sites over and over again when looking for a new or better job online. The Internet, however, is an extraordinarily dynamic medium, and successful online job search depends upon a continuous reassessment and updating of your site selections.

To conduct your evaluation, use both the lessons you've learned from previous job search efforts (see Step 4 above) and the Site Profiles in *Job Nation*. Based on your assessment, fine tune your selection of employment Websites every year or so. Why go to all that trouble? Because in today's challenging economic environment, you just never know when you may, once again, have to tap into the best employment sites on the Web.

The One Unranked Site That Deserves a Look

CareerFitness.com is a site designed to help you manage your job search AND your career successfully, in good economic times and bad. However, because it's based on Peter Weddle's book *Work Strong: Your Personal Career Fitness System*, it has not been included among the sites selected for *Job Nation*. Nevertheless, we at WEDDLE's strongly urge you to pay it a visit. You'll find everything you need to increase the paycheck and the satisfaction you bring home from work.

A One-of-a-Kind Site for Career Success

Today's job market is one of the most challenging in history. Tomorrow's job market will be no less so. In fact, the world of work has undergone a profound and permanent change since 2008. And, it will never again be the way that it was.

This new reality means that the old fashioned ways of finding a new or better job are now ineffective. The traditional strategies for achieving career success no longer work. What you used to be able to rely on for steady employment and advancement will set you back today and deny you access to opportunities tomorrow.

What should you do?

Visit **CareerFitness.com**. It's a state-of-the-art resource center for job search and career success. Think of it as your "Careerbook" page on the Web.

The site offers you an array of tools and techniques that will help you build up the strength, endurance and reach of your career. It will empower you to express and experience your unique talent in jobs that are meaningful and rewarding for you.

CareeFitness.com provides a complete toolkit for career success in today's world of work. It includes:

> A personal Career Fitness planning and status system so you can set up and keep track of everything you do for the health of your career and your success at work;

> Your very own Career Agent—an electronic image of yourself that will act as your online mentor, assistant, and cheerleader;

> Your own personal locker for storing your Career Fitness self-evaluations, your resume, your contacts and all of the other stuff you need to manage your job search and career effectively;

> Your own personal trophy case where you can keep track of and enjoy your career victories in the world of work (even if your boss overlooks them);

> A professional networking tool so you can expand your job search and career contacts and stay in touch with them regularly; and

> A resume builder so you can translate your career victories into a document that employers will understand and respect.

CareerFitness.com is a unique career self-management program specifically designed for the challenging workplace of the 21st Century. Visit the site today and get started on building your career fitness!

JOB NATION

The 100 Best Employment Sites on the Web

Notes

The 100 Best Employment Sites Cross Reference Index

The sites that are featured in *Job Nation* serve job seekers and career activists in a range of occupational fields, industries, and employment-related specialties (e.g., diversity, management). The following Cross Reference Index will help you quickly find the sites that best match your job search objectives and career goals.

Administrative/Clerical

BrokerHunter.com

DiversityJobs.com

HEALTHeCAREERS Network

Inside Higher Ed

Job.com

MinnesotaJobs.com

Net-Temps

RetirementJobs.com

VetJobs

Associations

AHACareerCenter.org (American Hospital Association)

JAMA Career Center® (American Medical Association)

ASAE Career Headquarters (American Society of Association Executives)

BlueSteps (Association of Executive Search Consultants)

DiversityConnect.com (National Urban League)

GARP Career Center (Global Association of Risk Professionals)

HEALTHeCAREERS Network (multiple associations)

IEEE Job Site (Institute of Electrical & Electronics Engineers)

JobsInBenefits.com (International Foundation of Employee Benefit Plans)

Marketing Career Network (multiple associations)

NACElink Network (National Association of Colleges & Employers)

National Healthcare Career Network (multiple associations)

NBMBAA Employment Network (National Black MBA Association)

PedJobs (American Academy of Pediatrics)

Physics Today Jobs (American Institute of Physics)

PRSA Jobcenter (Public Relations Society of America)

SHRM HRJobs (Society for Human Resource Management)

SPIE Career Center (The International Society for Optics & Photonics)

Banking/Securities

BrokerHunter.com

eFinancialCareers.com

GARP Career Center

WallStJobs.com

Biotechnology

AgCareers.com

BioSpace

Building Management

ApartmentCareers.com

Security Jobs Network™

Communications—All Media, Creative, Editorial

Coroflot

mediabistro.com

PRSA Jobcenter

TalentZoo.com

Construction

ConstructionJobs.com

MEP Jobs

Workopolis

Customer Service

AllRetailJobs.com

BrokerHunter.com

CallCenterJobs.com

Hcareers

LatPro

MinnesotaJobs.com

RetirementJobs.com

Sales Gravy

Work In Sports

Defense

ClearedConnections

MilitaryConnection.com

MilitaryHire.com

VetJobs

Diversity

disABLEDperson.com

DiversityConnect.com

DiversityJobs.com

LatPro

RetirementJobs.com

WorkplaceDiversity.com

Education

BioSpace

Careers in Proprietary Education

HigherEdJobs

Inside Higher Ed

Engineering

AfterCollege

Aviation Employment

ClearedConnections

CollegeRecruiter.com

ConstructionJobs.com

Dice.com

IEEE Job Site

JobsInLogistics.com

JobsInManufacturing.com

LatPro

MEP Jobs

MinnesotaJobs.com

Physics Today Jobs

RetirementJobs.com

SPIE Career Center

VetJobs

Entry Level

AfterCollege

CollegeRecruiter.com

NACElink Network

Executive Search/Staffing Support

BlueSteps

BountyJobs

Net-Temps

Finance & Accounting

Accounting Jobs Today

AfterCollege

BrokerHunter.com

eFinancialCareers.com

FINS from The Wall Street Journal

Hospital Jobs Online

Job.com

JobCircle.com

jobWings.com

LatPro

MinnesotaJobs.com

NBMBAA Employment Network

Net-Temps

RetirementJobs.com

6FigureJobs.com

SnagAJob.com

WallStJobs.com

General

AllCountyJobs.com

America's Job Exchange

BountyJobs

CareerBoard

CareerBuilder.com

Chicagojobs.com

disABLEDperson.com

DiversityConnect.com

FlexJobs

iHire.com

Indeed

Jobfox

Jobing.com

Job Rooster

JobsInME.com

JobsRadar

JobStreet.com Malaysia

JobTarget

MilitaryConnection.com

MilitaryHire.com

Monster.com

NACElink Network

NationJob.com

RegionalHelpWanted.com

Simply Hired

WorkplaceDiversity.com

Healthcare/Medical

Absolutely Health Care

AfterCollege

AHACareerCenter.org

AllHealthcareJobs.com

JAMA Career Center®

BioSpace

DiversityJobs.com

HEALTHeCAREERS Network

HealthJobsNationwide.com

Hospital Dream Jobs

Hospital Jobs Online

JobCircle.com

LiveCareer

National Healthcare Career Network

NursingJobs.org

PedJobs

Simply Hired

Workopolis

Hospitality

Cool Works

Hcareers

Meetingjobs

SnagAJob.com

Hourly

AllRetailJobs.com

Cool Works

JobsInManufacturing.com

SnagAJob.com

TopUSAJobs.com

Human Resources

Careers in Proprietary Education

DiversityJobs.com

EmployeeBenefitsJobs.com

ExecuNet

JobsInBenefits.com

SHRM HRJobs

Information Technology/Systems

AfterCollege

BrokerHunter.com

ClearedConnections

Dice.com

ExecuNet

FINS from The Wall Street Journal

IEEE Job Site

Job.com

JobCircle.com

mediabistro.com

MilitaryHire.com

MinnesotaJobs.com

Net-Temps

Physics Today Jobs

Simply Hired

6FigureJobs.com

SnagAJob.com

VetJobs

Workopolis

Insurance

Actuary.com

Great Insurance Jobs

Job Search/Career Advancement

BlueSteps

JobRooster

JobsRadar

LiveCareer

Logistics/Transportation

Aviation Employment

JobsInLogistics.com

JobsinTrucks.com

Management

AgCareers.com

AllHealthcareJobs.com

AllRetailJobs.com

ApartmentCareers.com

ASAE Career Headquarters

BlueSteps

BrokerHunter.com

CallCenterJobs.com

ClearedConnections

ConstructionJobs.com

Cool Works

ExecuNet

FINS from The Wall Street Journal

Hcareers

HealthJobsNationwide.com

Hospital Dream Jobs

IEEE Job Site

Inside Higher Ed

JobCircle.com

JobsInBenefits.com

JobsInLogistics.com

jobWings.com

mediabistro.com

NBMBAA Employment Network

Net-Temps

Sales Gravy

6FigureJobs.com

SnagAJob.com

VetJobs

WallStJobs.com

Work In Sports

Mathematics

Actuary.com

icrunchdata

Nonprofit

ASAE Career Headquarters

Opportunity Knocks

Operations

AgCareers.com

AllRetailJobs.com

ApartmentCareers.com

Aviation Employment

BrokerHunter.com

CallCenterJobs.com

ConstructionJobs.com

Hcareers

JobsInLogistics.com

NBMBAA Employment Network

6FigureJobs.com

SnagAJob.com

VetJobs

WallStJobs.com

Retail

AllRetailJobs.com

Net-Temps

SnagAJob.com

Sales & Marketing

AgCareers.com

AllRetailJobs.com

ASAE Career Headquarters

BrokerHunter.com

CallCenterJobs.com

Careers in Proprietary Education

CollegeRecruiter.com

ConstructionJobs.com

DiversityJobs.com

EHSCareers.com

ExecuNet

FINS from The Wall Street Journal

Great Insurance Jobs

Job.com

LatPro

Marketing Career Network

mediabistro.com

MinnesotaJobs.com

RetirementJobs.com

Sales Gravy

6FigureJobs.com

SnagAJob.com

TalentZoo.com

WallStJobs.com

Work In Sports

Workopolis

Science

AfterCollege

BioSpace

IEEE Job Site

Physics Today Jobs

SPIE Career Center

Search Engines—Employment

Indeed

Juju.com

Simply Hired

TopUSAJobs.com

Specialty—Other

AgCareers.com

America's Job Exchange

Aviation Employment

CallCenterJobs.com

ClearedConnections

Cool Works

Coroflot

disABLEDperson.com

EHSCareers.com

FlexJobs

JobsInManufacturing.com

Meetingjobs

Work In Sports

Temporary/Contract Employment

Net-Temps

SnagAJob.com

USA—By Region/Time Zone

Eastern Time Zone (AL, AK, DE, FL, GA, MA, MD, MI, NC, NJ, NY, OH, PA)

AllCountyJobs.com

CareerBoard

JobCircle.com

Jobing.com

JobsInME.com

RegionalHelpWanted.com

WallStJobs.com

Central (IL, IA, KS, KY, LA, MN, MO, ND, NE, OK, SD, TN, TX, WI)

CareerBoard

Chicagojobs.com

Jobing.com

MinnesotaJobs.com

RegionalHelpWanted.com

Mountain Time Zone (AZ, CO, ID, NM, UT)

CareerBoard

Jobing.com

RegionalHelpWanted.com

Western Time Zone (CA, NV, OR, WA)

CareerBoard

Jobing.com

RegionalHelpWanted.com

Canada

AllRetailJobs.com

Great Insurance Jobs

Hcareers

HEALTHeCAREERS Network

JobsInLogistics.com

JobsInManufacturing.com

jobWings.com

RegionalHelpWanted.com

Workopolis

Absolutely Health Care
www.healthjobsusa.com
CJ Ventures, Inc.

GENERAL SITE INFORMATION

Date activated online:	1999
Location of site headquarters:	Lake Worth, FL
Number of people who visit the site:	631,909 unique visitors/month
Time spent on site:	10.6 page views/visitor

JOB POSTINGS

Post full time jobs:	Yes
Post part time/contract/consulting jobs:	Yes - All
Most prevalent types of jobs posted:	Healthcare, Medical
Distribution:	National - USA
Number of job postings:	345,000
Top salary levels of jobs:	$201-250K, $251K+/yr
Source of postings:	Employers, Staffing

RESUME SERVICES

Are resumes or profiles posted on the site:	Yes
How long can you store:	Indefinitely
Who can post a resume:	Those in the field
Fee to post:	None
Confidentiality available:	No

OTHER SERVICES

Is a listserv or discussion forum offered:	Yes
Are assessment instruments offered:	Yes
Automated job agent:	Yes
Career info provided:	Yes
Links to other sites:	Yes

SITE'S SELF DESCRIPTION

Absolutely Health Care specializes in U.S. healthcare and medical positions. We offer single job postings and programs that allow unlimited postings and resume database access. Jobs posted by our clients are also cross posted to 4,800+ affiliate sites at no extra charge. Unlimited postings and resume database access average $333 per month for annual subscribers.

Contact Information

Name: Ken Levinson
Phone: 800-863-8314   E-Mail: klevinson@healthjobsusa.com

Accounting Jobs Today
www.accountingjobstoday.com
Internet Brands, Inc.

GENERAL SITE INFORMATION

Date activated online:	2007
Location of site headquarters:	El Segundo, CA
Number of people who visit the site:	50,000 unique visitors/month
Time spent on site:	3.0 page views/visitor

JOB POSTINGS

Post full time jobs:	Yes
Post part time/contract/consulting jobs:	No
Most prevalent types of jobs posted:	FA
Distribution:	National - USAA
Number of job postings:	3,000
Top salary levels of jobs:	Not Reported
Source of postings:	Employers

RESUME SERVICES

Are resumes or profiles posted on the site:	Yes
How long can you store:	Indefinitely
Who can post a resume:	Those in the field
Fee to post:	None
Confidentiality available:	Yes

OTHER SERVICES

Is a listserv or discussion forum offered:	No
Are assessment instruments offered:	Yes
Automated job agent:	Yes
Career info provided:	Yes
Links to other sites:	Yes

SITE'S SELF DESCRIPTION

AccountingJobsToday.com is an accounting job board and career resource dedicated to accounting and finance professionals nationwide. For employers and recruiters, we connect you with highly targeted and quality talent. Post your jobs on AccountingJobsToday.com or search our extensive and growing pool of talented job seekers via our resume database.

Contact Information

Name: Steve Gilison
Phone: 310-280-5529   E-Mail: advertising@accountingjobstoday.com

Actuary.com

www.actuary.com
RSG, Inc.

GENERAL SITE INFORMATION

Date activated online:	1999
Location of site headquarters:	Atlanta, GA
Number of people who visit the site:	40,000 unique visitors/month
Time spent on site:	3:30 minutes/visit

JOB POSTINGS

Post full time jobs:	Yes
Post part time/contract/consulting jobs:	Yes - All
Most prevalent types of jobs posted:	Actuarial, Insurance, Mathematics
Distribution:	International
Number of job postings:	100
Top salary levels of jobs:	$201-250K, $251K+/yr
Source of postings:	Employers, Staffing

RESUME SERVICES

Are resumes or profiles posted on the site:	Yes
How long can you store:	Indefinitely
Who can post a resume:	Anyone
Fee to post:	None
Confidentiality available:	Yes

OTHER SERVICES

Is a listserv or discussion forum offered:	Yes
Are assessment instruments offered:	Yes
Automated job agent:	Yes
Career info provided:	Yes
Links to other sites:	Yes

SITE'S SELF DESCRIPTION

Actuary.com is the leading career and professional resource for actuaries on the Internet. Actuary.com offers single job postings from $225 or job posting packs at a significant price reduction. Top name actuarial companies have posted on Actuary.com for years.

Contact Information

Name: Jay Rollins
Phone: 770-425-8576   E-Mail: actuary@actuary.com

AfterCollege
www.aftercollege.com
AfterCollege, Inc.

GENERAL SITE INFORMATION

Date activated online:	2000
Location of site headquarters:	San Francisco, CA
Number of people who visit the site:	600,000 unique visitors/month
Time spent on site:	15.0 page views/visitor

JOB POSTINGS

Post full time jobs:	Yes
Post part time/contract/consulting jobs:	Yes - Part time
Most prevalent types of jobs posted:	EN, IS, Business, Life Sciences, Nursing
Distribution:	National - USA
Number of job postings:	177,008
Top salary levels of jobs:	$101-150K/yr
Source of postings:	Employers

RESUME SERVICES

Are resumes or profiles posted on the site:	Yes - Both
How long can you store:	Indefinitely
Who can post a resume:	Active members
Fee to post:	None
Confidentiality available:	Yes

OTHER SERVICES

Is a listserv or discussion forum offered:	No
Are assessment instruments offered:	Yes
Automated job agent:	Yes
Career info provided:	Yes
Links to other sites:	Yes

SITE'S SELF DESCRIPTION

AfterCollege is the largest career network specializing in college recruitment, helping over 2,250,000 college students and alumni connect with employers. AfterCollege reaches students and alumni through 1,300 partner academic departments and student groups as well as through a network of 17,500+ faculty and group contacts.

Contact Information

Name: Carrie McCullagh
Phone: 877-725-7721   E-Mail: info@aftercollege.com

AgCareers.com
www.agcareers.com
Farms.com

GENERAL SITE INFORMATION

Date activated online: January, 2001
Location of site headquarters: Clinton, NC
Number of people who visit the site: 48,600 unique visitors/month
Time spent on site: 4:30 minutes/visit

JOB POSTINGS

Post full time jobs: Yes
Post part time/contract/consulting jobs: Yes - All
Most prevalent types of jobs posted: Agriculture
Distribution: International
Number of job postings: 2,750
Top salary levels of jobs: $76-100K, $101-150K/yr
Source of postings: Employers, Staffing

RESUME SERVICES

Are resumes or profiles posted on the site: Yes
How long can you store: 1 year
Who can post a resume: Those registered
Fee to post: None
Confidentiality available: Yes

OTHER SERVICES

Is a listserv or discussion forum offered: Yes
Are assessment instruments offered: No
Automated job agent: Yes
Career info provided: Yes
Links to other sites: Yes

SITE'S SELF DESCRIPTION

AgCareers.com is the leading online job board and human resource provider for the agriculture, food, natural resources and biotechnology fields.

Contact Information

Name: AgCareers.com
Phone: 800-929-8975   E-Mail: agcareers@agcareers.com

AHACareerCenter.org
www.ahacareercenter.org
AHA Solutions, Inc. (American Hospital Association)

GENERAL SITE INFORMATION

Date activated online:	November, 2007
Location of site headquarters:	Chicago, IL
Number of people who visit the site:	8,031 unique visitors/month
Time spent on site:	2:57 minutes/visit

JOB POSTINGS

Post full time jobs:	Yes
Post part time/contract/consulting jobs:	Yes - Locum Tenens
Most prevalent types of jobs posted:	Healthcare
Distribution:	National - USA
Number of job postings:	1,600
Top salary levels of jobs:	Up to $200K+/yr
Source of postings:	Employers

RESUME SERVICES

Are resumes or profiles posted on the site:	Yes
How long can you store:	Indefinitely
Who can post a resume:	Those registered
Fee to post:	None
Confidentiality available:	Yes

OTHER SERVICES

Is a listserv or discussion forum offered:	No
Are assessment instruments offered:	No
Automated job agent:	Yes
Career info provided:	Yes
Links to other sites:	Yes

SITE'S SELF DESCRIPTION

AHA's Career Center is the site for hospitals and healthcare employers seeking highly qualified applicants (from entry level to CEO), as well as job seekers looking to land the right job within healthcare. The American Hospital Association's AHACareerCenter.org is part of the National Healthcare Career Network and the fastest growing health care association job network.

Contact Information

Name: Amy Goble
Phone: 800-242-4677   E-Mail: careercenter@aha.org

AllCountyJobs.com
www.allcountyjobs.com
AllCountyJobs, LLC

GENERAL SITE INFORMATION

Date activated online:	1999
Location of site headquarters:	Trumbull, CT
Number of people who visit the site:	250,000 unique visitors/month
Time spent on site:	6:00 minutes/visit

JOB POSTINGS

Post full time jobs:	Yes
Post part time/contract/consulting jobs:	Yes - All
Most prevalent types of jobs posted:	Wide variety
Distribution:	Regional - CT, NY, MA, RI, NJ, VT, NH
Number of job postings:	3,000
Top salary levels of jobs:	Up to $150K+/yr
Source of postings:	Employers, Staffing

RESUME SERVICES

Are resumes or profiles posted on the site:	Yes
How long can you store:	2 years
Who can post a resume:	Those registered
Fee to post:	None
Confidentiality available:	Yes

OTHER SERVICES

Is a listserv or discussion forum offered:	No
Are assessment instruments offered:	No
Automated job agent:	No
Career info provided:	No
Links to other sites:	No

SITE'S SELF DESCRIPTION

We are a network of local online job boards. Since our start, we have always strived for one goal: connect employers with quality, targeted, local applicants. Our local job boards will let you search/post jobs from Washington, D.C. to Vermont and everywhere in between. Each site links to the others to form a network of thousands of job listings along the East Coast.

Contact Information

Name: Information
Phone: 800-399-6651   E-Mail: info@allcountyjobs.com

AllHealthcareJobs.com
www.allhealthcarejobs.com
Dice Holdings, Inc.

GENERAL SITE INFORMATION

Date activated online:	2005
Location of site headquarters:	New York, NY
Number of people who visit the site:	243,000 unique visitors/month
Time spent on site:	8:00 minutes/visit

JOB POSTINGS

Post full time jobs:	Yes
Post part time/contract/consulting jobs:	Yes - Part time
Most prevalent types of jobs posted:	MG, Nursing, Allied Health
Distribution:	International
Number of job postings:	15,000
Top salary levels of jobs:	$101-150K, $251K+/yr
Source of postings:	Employers, Staffing

RESUME SERVICES

Are resumes or profiles posted on the site:	Yes
How long can you store:	Indefinitely
Who can post a resume:	Those in the field
Fee to post:	None
Confidentiality available:	Yes

OTHER SERVICES

Is a listserv or discussion forum offered:	No
Are assessment instruments offered:	No
Automated job agent:	Yes
Career info provided:	Yes
Links to other sites:	Yes

SITE'S SELF DESCRIPTION

AllHealthcareJobs.com, a Dice Holdings, Inc. service, is a leading online career site dedicated to matching healthcare professionals with the best career opportunities in their profession. Recruiters and employers can post jobs targeting specific fields within the healthcare industry including allied health, nursing, laboratory, pharmacy and medicine.

Contact Information

Name: Tim Stene
Phone: 515-313-2069   E-Mail: tim.stene@allhealthcarejobs.com

AllRetailJobs.com
www.allretailjobs.com
JobsInLogistics.com, Inc.

GENERAL SITE INFORMATION

Date activated online:	2001
Location of site headquarters:	North Miami Beach, FL
Number of people who visit the site:	750,000 unique visitors/month
Time spent on site:	5.0 page views/visitor

JOB POSTINGS

Post full time jobs:	Yes
Post part time/contract/consulting jobs:	Yes - All
Most prevalent types of jobs posted:	MG, SM, Customer Service
Distribution:	USA, Canada
Number of job postings:	55,000
Top salary levels of jobs:	$151-200K/yr
Source of postings:	Employers, Staffing

RESUME SERVICES

Are resumes or profiles posted on the site:	Yes
How long can you store:	1 year
Who can post a resume:	Anyone
Fee to post:	None
Confidentiality available:	Yes

OTHER SERVICES

Is a listserv or discussion forum offered:	No
Are assessment instruments offered:	No
Automated job agent:	Yes
Career info provided:	Yes
Links to other sites:	Yes

SITE'S SELF DESCRIPTION

AllRetailJobs.com is the largest recruiting job board for the retail industry. The site specializes in target marketing campaigns that attract retail executives, regional managers, store and assistant store managers, category managers/buyers, retail logistics managers, merchandisers and department managers as well as sales and hourly associates.

Contact Information

Name: Amy Noah
Phone: 877-562-7368   E-Mail: amy@allretailjobs.com

America's Job Exchange
www.americasjobexchange.com
America's Job Exchange

GENERAL SITE INFORMATION

Date activated online:	June, 2007
Location of site headquarters:	Andover, MA
Number of people who visit the site:	1,250,000 unique visitors/month
Time spent on site:	4:00 minutes/visit

JOB POSTINGS

Post full time jobs:	Yes
Post part time/contract/consulting jobs:	No
Most prevalent types of jobs posted:	Wide variety
Distribution:	National - USA
Number of job postings:	500,000
Top salary levels of jobs:	Up to $80K/yr
Source of postings:	Employers

RESUME SERVICES

Are resumes or profiles posted on the site:	Yes
How long can you store:	Indefinitely
Who can post a resume:	Those registered
Fee to post:	None
Confidentiality available:	Yes

OTHER SERVICES

Is a listserv or discussion forum offered:	Yes
Are assessment instruments offered:	Yes
Automated job agent:	Yes
Career info provided:	Yes
Links to other sites:	Yes

SITE'S SELF DESCRIPTION

America's Job Exchange (AJE) provides search, job listings and career tools to help job seekers be successful in their job hunting and career growth. In addition, the AJE network offers specialized Web-sites for niche communities, such as veterans, seniors, disabled, minorities and many more to make the job search experience more personalized and effective.

Contact Information

Name: Rathin Sinha
Phone: 866-923-6284   E-Mail: customercare@americasjobexchange.com

ApartmentCareers.com
www.apartmentcareers.com
Realestatecareers, LLC

GENERAL SITE INFORMATION

Date activated online:	2000
Location of site headquarters:	Dallas, TX
Number of people who visit the site:	50,000 unique visitors/month
Time spent on site:	10.0 page views/visitor

JOB POSTINGS

Post full time jobs:	Yes
Post part time/contract/consulting jobs:	Yes - All
Most prevalent types of jobs posted:	On-site apartment staff
Distribution:	National - USA
Number of job postings:	250+
Top salary levels of jobs:	$101-150K/yr
Source of postings:	Employers

RESUME SERVICES

Are resumes or profiles posted on the site:	Yes
How long can you store:	Indefinitely
Who can post a resume:	Anyone
Fee to post:	None
Confidentiality available:	Yes

OTHER SERVICES

Is a listserv or discussion forum offered:	Yes
Are assessment instruments offered:	Yes
Automated job agent:	Yes
Career info provided:	Yes
Links to other sites:	Yes

SITE'S SELF DESCRIPTION

ApartmentCareers.com is the largest career site dedicated to advertising the staffing needs of the apartment industry. The National Apartment Association (NAA), the largest rental housing association in the U.S., selected ApartmentCareers.com to host the NAA Career Center and develop a nationwide network of association career sites to meet the needs of its 50,000 members.

Contact Information

Name: John Cullens
Phone: 972-692-2430   E-Mail: info@apartmentcareers.com

ASAE Career Headquarters

www.careerhq.org
American Society of Association Executives (ASAE)

GENERAL SITE INFORMATION

Date activated online:	2000
Location of site headquarters:	Washington, D.C.
Number of people who visit the site:	35,000 unique visitors/month
Time spent on site:	6.2 page views/visitor

JOB POSTINGS

Post full time jobs:	Yes
Post part time/contract/consulting jobs:	Yes - All
Most prevalent types of jobs posted:	MG, SM, Association Executive/Manager
Distribution:	National - USA
Number of job postings:	400
Top salary levels of jobs:	$51-75K, $101-150K/yr
Source of postings:	Employers, Staffing

RESUME SERVICES

Are resumes or profiles posted on the site:	Yes
How long can you store:	Indefinitely
Who can post a resume:	Anyone
Fee to post:	None
Confidentiality available:	Yes

OTHER SERVICES

Is a listserv or discussion forum offered:	No
Are assessment instruments offered:	No
Automated job agent:	Yes
Career info provided:	Yes
Links to other sites:	Yes

SITE'S SELF DESCRIPTION

ASAE's CareerHQ.org is the largest source of association industry jobs and resumes. It's where job seekers go to land the right job, and where employers go to find highly qualified applicants. CareerHQ.org also offers career development services, a mentoring program, and salary tables to help job seekers increase their competitive advantage.

Contact Information

Name: Catherine Lux Fry
Phone: 202-626-2819

E-Mail: clux@asaecenter.org

Aviation Employment
www.aviationmployment.com
Internet Brands, Inc.

GENERAL SITE INFORMATION

Date activated online:	1996
Location of site headquarters:	El Segundo, CA
Number of people who visit the site:	50,000 unique visitors/month
Time spent on site:	5:00 minutes/visit

JOB POSTINGS

Post full time jobs:	Yes
Post part time/contract/consulting jobs:	Yes - All
Most prevalent types of jobs posted:	A&P Mechanic, Engineer, Maintenance
Distribution:	International
Number of job postings:	1,000
Top salary levels of jobs:	Not Reported
Source of postings:	Employers

RESUME SERVICES

Are resumes or profiles posted on the site:	Yes
How long can you store:	Indefinitely
Who can post a resume:	Those registered
Fee to post:	None
Confidentiality available:	Yes

OTHER SERVICES

Is a listserv or discussion forum offered:	Yes
Are assessment instruments offered:	No
Automated job agent:	Yes
Career info provided:	Yes
Links to other sites:	Yes

SITE'S SELF DESCRIPTION

Since 1996, AviationEmployment.com has helped millions of aviation and aerospace professionals find career opportunities. We specialize in the areas of aviation maintenance, engineering, A&P mechanic and avionics jobs. We are the #1 search result on Google for the keyword "aviation jobs." Unlike our competition, we never charge job seekers to post resumes.

Contact Information

Name: Sales
Phone: 800-573-1848   E-Mail: jobs@aviationemployment.com

BioSpace
www.biospace.com
onTargetjobs, Inc.

GENERAL SITE INFORMATION

Date activated online:	1985
Location of site headquarters:	Englewood, CO
Number of people who visit the site:	311,282 unique visitors/month
Time spent on site:	5:00 minutes/visit

JOB POSTINGS

Post full time jobs:	Yes
Post part time/contract/consulting jobs:	Yes - All
Most prevalent types of jobs posted:	Biotech, Pharma, Med Device, Academic
Distribution:	International
Number of job postings:	3,000
Top salary levels of jobs:	$51-75K, $76-100K/yr
Source of postings:	Employers

RESUME SERVICES

Are resumes or profiles posted on the site:	Yes
How long can you store:	1 year
Who can post a resume:	Those registered
Fee to post:	None
Confidentiality available:	Yes

OTHER SERVICES

Is a listserv or discussion forum offered:	Yes
Are assessment instruments offered:	No
Automated job agent:	Yes
Career info provided:	Yes
Links to other sites:	Yes

SITE'S SELF DESCRIPTION

BioSpace provides employment and career resources that span the life sciences. Unlike general job boards, our leading partnerships allow us to reach niche audiences within clinical research, academia, medical device sectors, government markets and other areas. More than 75% of BioSpace.com visitors return within a week, and another 90% don't visit other industry sites.

Contact Information

Name: Joe Kroog
Phone: 303-562-0351   E-Mail: joe.kroog@biospace.com

BlueSteps

www.bluesteps.com
Association of Executive Search Consultants (AESC)

GENERAL SITE INFORMATION

Date activated online:	November, 2000
Location of site headquarters:	New York, NY
Number of people who visit the site:	40,000 unique visitors/month
Time spent on site:	4:00 minutes/visit

JOB POSTINGS

Post full time jobs:	No
Post part time/contract/consulting jobs:	No
Most prevalent types of jobs posted:	N/A
Distribution:	N/A
Number of job postings:	N/A
Top salary levels of jobs:	N/A
Source of postings:	N/A

RESUME SERVICES

Are resumes or profiles posted on the site:	Yes
How long can you store:	Indefinitely
Who can post a resume:	Those registered
Fee to post:	$329
Confidentiality available:	Yes

OTHER SERVICES

Is a listserv or discussion forum offered:	No
Are assessment instruments offered:	No
Automated job agent:	No
Career info provided:	Yes
Links to other sites:	Yes

SITE'S SELF DESCRIPTION

As a service of the Association of Executive Search Consultants (AESC), BlueSteps gives senior executives direct visibility to over 6,000 executive recruiters at the top executive search firms worldwide. All firms are members of the AESC, the globally recognized body representing the retained executive search profession.

Contact Information

Name: Customer Support
Phone: 800-363-1207   E-Mail: info@bluesteps.com

BountyJobs

www.bountyjobs.com
BountyJobs, Inc.

GENERAL SITE INFORMATION

Date activated online:	November, 2006
Location of site headquarters:	New York, NY
Number of people who visit the site:	25,000 unique visitors/month
Time spent on site:	5:00 minutes/visit

JOB POSTINGS

Post full time jobs:	Yes
Post part time/contract/consulting jobs:	No
Most prevalent types of jobs posted:	Wide variety
Distribution:	International
Number of job postings:	2,000+
Top salary levels of jobs:	$76-100K, $180-220K/yr
Source of postings:	Employers, Staffing

RESUME SERVICES

Are resumes or profiles posted on the site:	No
How long can you store:	N/A
Who can post a resume:	N/A
Fee to post:	N/A
Confidentiality available:	N/A

OTHER SERVICES

Is a listserv or discussion forum offered:	No
Are assessment instruments offered:	No
Automated job agent:	No
Career info provided:	No
Links to other sites:	No

SITE'S SELF DESCRIPTION

BountyJobs is an online marketplace that connects employers with a national network of seasoned headhunters in seconds. Rather than being chained to the phone with headhunters all day, BountyJobs guarantees efficient collaboration with the headhunter channel through a single Web-based application. BountyJobs is the preferred contingent search solution.

Contact Information

Name: Employers Information
Phone: 212-660-3960   E-Mail: employers@bountyjobs.com

BrokerHunter.com
www.brokerhunter.com
BrokerHunter.com, LLC

GENERAL SITE INFORMATION

Date activated online:	2000
Location of site headquarters:	Cumming, GA
Number of people who visit the site:	170,000 unique visitors/month
Time spent on site:	5:33 minutes/visit

JOB POSTINGS

Post full time jobs:	Yes
Post part time/contract/consulting jobs:	Yes - All
Most prevalent types of jobs posted:	AD, FA, IS, OP, SM, Customer Service
Distribution:	International
Number of job postings:	8,183
Top salary levels of jobs:	Up to $251K+/yr
Source of postings:	Employers, Staffing

RESUME SERVICES

Are resumes or profiles posted on the site:	No
How long can you store:	Indefinitely
Who can post a resume:	Those registered
Fee to post:	None
Confidentiality available:	Yes

OTHER SERVICES

Is a listserv or discussion forum offered:	Yes
Are assessment instruments offered:	No
Automated job agent:	Yes
Career info provided:	Yes
Links to other sites:	Yes

SITE'S SELF DESCRIPTION

BrokerHunter.com is the leading securities industry employment Web-site in the nation with over 145,000 candidates and over 8,000 job postings from hundreds of branches and firms. The company's area of expertise is in the gathering and presentation of highly tailored data related to securities industry job seekers and to financial services employers and recruiters.

Contact Information

Name: Steve Testerman
Phone: 770-781-2629 x200   E-Mail: sales@brokerhunter.com

CallCenterJobs.com
www.callcenterjobs.com
CallCenterJobs.com

GENERAL SITE INFORMATION

Date activated online:	1999
Location of site headquarters:	Omaha, NE
Number of people who visit the site:	143,000+ unique visitors/month
Time spent on site:	3:23 minutes/visit

JOB POSTINGS

Post full time jobs:	Yes
Post part time/contract/consulting jobs:	Yes - Part time
Most prevalent types of jobs posted:	MG, OP, SM, Customer Service
Distribution:	National - USA
Number of job postings:	550
Top salary levels of jobs:	Up to $130+K/yr
Source of postings:	Employers

RESUME SERVICES

Are resumes or profiles posted on the site:	Yes
How long can you store:	2 years
Who can post a resume:	Anyone
Fee to post:	None
Confidentiality available:	Yes

OTHER SERVICES

Is a listserv or discussion forum offered:	No
Are assessment instruments offered:	Yes
Automated job agent:	Yes
Career info provided:	Yes
Links to other sites:	Yes

SITE'S SELF DESCRIPTION

CallCenterJobs.com specializes in contact center, customer service, telesales, help desk and collections positions. We provide quality jobs and attract quality employment candidates who are not visiting the larger job boards. We also provide a directory of industry resources to provide professionals with an extensive collection of online call center resources.

Contact Information

Name: Jim Moylan
Phone: 880-353-7529   E-Mail: jm@callcenterjobs.com

CareerBoard
www.careerboard.com
JobServe USA

GENERAL SITE INFORMATION

Date activated online:	May, 1997
Location of site headquarters:	Beachwood, OH
Number of people who visit the site:	185,000 unique visitors/month
Time spent on site:	3.8 page views/visitor

JOB POSTINGS

Post full time jobs:	Yes
Post part time/contract/consulting jobs:	Yes - All
Most prevalent types of jobs posted:	Wide variety
Distribution:	National - USA
Number of job postings:	16,000
Top salary levels of jobs:	$76-100K, $101-150K/yr
Source of postings:	Employers, Staffing

RESUME SERVICES

Are resumes or profiles posted on the site:	Yes
How long can you store:	2 years
Who can post a resume:	Those registered
Fee to post:	None
Confidentiality available:	Yes

OTHER SERVICES

Is a listserv or discussion forum offered:	No
Are assessment instruments offered:	Yes
Automated job agent:	Yes
Career info provided:	Yes
Links to other sites:	Yes

SITE'S SELF DESCRIPTION

CareerBoard connects local employers with local job seekers. Our nationwide network of niche and sixty-eight geographically targeted local employment Web-sites ensures jobs are seen by the most relevant job seekers wherever they are located. Our network reaches 32 million unique visitors/month and produces quality response to postings in all categories and USA locations.

Contact Information

Name: CareerBoard
Phone: 877-619-5627   E-Mail: careerboard@careerboard.com

CareerBuilder.com
www.careerbuilder.com
CareerBuilder, LLC

GENERAL SITE INFORMATION

Date activated online:	1998
Location of site headquarters:	Chicago, IL
Number of people who visit the site:	25,000,000 unique visitors/month
Time spent on site:	12:00+ minutes/visit

JOB POSTINGS

Post full time jobs:	Yes
Post part time/contract/consulting jobs:	Yes - All
Most prevalent types of jobs posted:	Wide variety
Distribution:	International
Number of job postings:	1,000,000+
Top salary levels of jobs:	Not Reported
Source of postings:	Employers, Staffing

RESUME SERVICES

Are resumes or profiles posted on the site:	Yes
How long can you store:	Indefinitely
Who can post a resume:	Anyone
Fee to post:	None
Confidentiality available:	Yes

OTHER SERVICES

Is a listserv or discussion forum offered:	Yes
Are assessment instruments offered:	Yes
Automated job agent:	Yes
Career info provided:	Yes
Links to other sites:	Yes

SITE'S SELF DESCRIPTION

CareerBuilder.com is the nation's largest online job site with more than 25 million unique visitors and over one million jobs. Owned by Gannett Co., Inc. (NYSE:GCI), Tribune Company, The McClatchy Company (NYSE:MNI) and Microsoft Corp. (Nasdaq: MSFT), the company offers a vast online and print network to help job seekers connect with employers.

Contact Information

Name: Customer Service
Phone: 800-891-8880   E-Mail: Not Reported

Careers in Proprietary Education

www.propedu.com
Careers in Proprietary Education, Inc.

GENERAL SITE INFORMATION

Date activated online:	January, 2011
Location of site headquarters:	Coconut Creek, FL
Number of people who visit the site:	1,700 unique visitors/month
Time spent on site:	4:34 minutes/visit

JOB POSTINGS

Post full time jobs:	Yes
Post part time/contract/consulting jobs:	Yes - Part time, Adjunct Faculty
Most prevalent types of jobs posted:	Campus Director, Academic Dean
Distribution:	National - USA
Number of job postings:	118
Top salary levels of jobs:	Up to $125K+/yr
Source of postings:	Employers

RESUME SERVICES

Are resumes or profiles posted on the site:	Yes
How long can you store:	Indefinitely
Who can post a resume:	Those registered
Fee to post:	None
Confidentiality available:	Yes

OTHER SERVICES

Is a listserv or discussion forum offered:	Yes
Are assessment instruments offered:	Yes
Automated job agent:	Yes
Career info provided:	No
Links to other sites:	Yes

SITE'S SELF DESCRIPTION

Careers in Proprietary Education is a niche site dedicated to the proprietary education industry. It links professionals with careers in proprietary education and provides for-profit and non-profit K-12 schools, colleges, universities and institutes with exceptional talent.

Contact Information

Name: Susan Forman
Phone: 954-596-8100   E-Mail: susan@propedu.com

Chicagojobs.com
www.chicagojobs.com
Shaker Recruitment Advertising & Communications

GENERAL SITE INFORMATION

Date activated online:	2004
Location of site headquarters:	Chicago, IL
Number of people who visit the site:	150,000 unique visitors/month
Time spent on site:	30.0 page views/visitor

JOB POSTINGS

Post full time jobs:	Yes
Post part time/contract/consulting jobs:	Yes - All
Most prevalent types of jobs posted:	Wide variety
Distribution:	Regional/USA: Chicago, IL
Number of job postings:	5,000+
Top salary levels of jobs:	$31-50K, $51-75K/yr
Source of postings:	Employers

RESUME SERVICES

Are resumes or profiles posted on the site:	Yes
How long can you store:	Indefinitely
Who can post a resume:	Anyone
Fee to post:	None
Confidentiality available:	Yes

OTHER SERVICES

Is a listserv or discussion forum offered:	No
Are assessment instruments offered:	No
Automated job agent:	Yes
Career info provided:	Yes
Links to other sites:	Yes

SITE'S SELF DESCRIPTION

Exclusively focused on Chicagoland's 11 county area including the city, suburbs and beyond, ChicagoJobs.com's award-winning layout and enhanced services maximize exposure for both local employers and job seekers. Launched in 2004, we average 150,000 unique monthly visitors and more than 4.5 million page views each month.

Contact Information

Name: Sales
Phone: 877-562-7244   E-Mail: sales@chicagojobs.com

ClearedConnections
www.clearedconnections.com
Cleared People, LLC

GENERAL SITE INFORMATION

Date activated online:	November, 1999
Location of site headquarters:	Reston, VA
Number of people who visit the site:	145,000+ unique visitors/month
Time spent on site:	8:10 minutes/visit

JOB POSTINGS

Post full time jobs:	Yes
Post part time/contract/consulting jobs:	Yes - All
Most prevalent types of jobs posted:	EN, IS, MG, Government
Distribution:	International
Number of job postings:	5,000
Top salary levels of jobs:	Up to $195K/yr
Source of postings:	Employers

RESUME SERVICES

Are resumes or profiles posted on the site:	Yes
How long can you store:	Indefinitely
Who can post a resume:	Only those in field
Fee to post:	None
Confidentiality available:	Yes

OTHER SERVICES

Is a listserv or discussion forum offered:	Yes
Are assessment instruments offered:	No
Automated job agent:	Yes
Career info provided:	Yes
Links to other sites:	Yes

SITE'S SELF DESCRIPTION

Serving over one hundred federal contractors, ClearedConnections is an online resource for security cleared professionals. Its focus is to identify individuals with an active security clearance and facilitate an introduction to organizations with corresponding hiring requirements. ClearedConnections exclusively connects cleared personnel with cleared facilities (FCL's).

Contact Information

Name: Robert Esti
Phone: 703-860-2246   E-Mail: robert@clearedconnections.com

CollegeRecruiter.com
www.collegerecruiter.com
CollegeRecruiter.com

GENERAL SITE INFORMATION

Date activated online:	1996
Location of site headquarters:	Minneapolis, MN
Number of people who visit the site:	500,000 unique visitors/month
Time spent on site:	3.0 page views/visitor

JOB POSTINGS

Post full time jobs:	Yes
Post part time/contract/consulting jobs:	Yes - All
Most prevalent types of jobs posted:	EN, SM, Internships
Distribution:	National - USA
Number of job postings:	700,000
Top salary levels of jobs:	$201-250K, $251K+/yr
Source of postings:	Employers, Other sites

RESUME SERVICES

Are resumes or profiles posted on the site:	No
How long can you store:	N/A
Who can post a resume:	N/A
Fee to post:	N/A
Confidentiality available:	N/A

OTHER SERVICES

Is a listserv or discussion forum offered:	Yes
Are assessment instruments offered:	Yes
Automated job agent:	Yes
Career info provided:	Yes
Links to other sites:	Yes

SITE'S SELF DESCRIPTION

CollegeRecruiter.com is the leading job board for college students searching for internships and recent graduates hunting for entry-level and other career opportunities. Features tens of thousands of pages of employment-related articles, blogs, videos, podcasts and other such content.

Contact Information

Name: Steven Rothberg
Phone: 952-848-2211   E-Mail: steven@collegerecruiter.com

ConstructionJobs.com

www.constructionjobs.com
Construction Jobs, Inc.

GENERAL SITE INFORMATION

Date activated online:	2000
Location of site headquarters:	Asheville, NC
Number of people who visit the site:	165,000 unique visitors/month
Time spent on site:	2.3 page views/visitor

JOB POSTINGS

Post full time jobs:	Yes
Post part time/contract/consulting jobs:	Yes - All
Most prevalent types of jobs posted:	EN, MG, OP, SM
Distribution:	National - USA
Number of job postings:	1,700
Top salary levels of jobs:	$101-150K/yr
Source of postings:	Employers, Staffing

RESUME SERVICES

Are resumes or profiles posted on the site:	Yes
How long can you store:	6 months
Who can post a resume:	Anyone
Fee to post:	None
Confidentiality available:	Yes

OTHER SERVICES

Is a listserv or discussion forum offered:	No
Are assessment instruments offered:	Yes
Automated job agent:	Yes
Career info provided:	Yes
Links to other sites:	Yes

SITE'S SELF DESCRIPTION

ConstructionJobs.com is the nation's premier employment resource for the construction, design and building industries. Endorsed by 9 industry associations as their preferred partner for online recruiting, our award-winning job board and resume database provide a cost-effective solution that makes advertising openings and locating qualified candidates faster and easier.

Contact Information

Name: Alan Kerschen
Phone: 828-251-1344   E-Mail: info@constructionjobs.com

Cool Works
www.coolworks.com
CW, Inc.

GENERAL SITE INFORMATION

Date activated online:	November, 1995
Location of site headquarters:	Gardiner, MT
Number of people who visit the site:	108,500 unique visitors/month
Time spent on site:	4:11 minutes/visit

JOB POSTINGS

Post full time jobs:	Yes
Post part time/contract/consulting jobs:	Yes - Seasonal jobs
Most prevalent types of jobs posted:	MG, Food and beverage, Housekeeping
Distribution:	National - USA
Number of job postings:	35+
Top salary levels of jobs:	Hourly, $20-100K/yr
Source of postings:	Employers

RESUME SERVICES

Are resumes or profiles posted on the site:	No
How long can you store:	N/A
Who can post a resume:	N/A
Fee to post:	N/A
Confidentiality available:	N/A

OTHER SERVICES

Is a listserv or discussion forum offered:	Yes
Are assessment instruments offered:	No
Automated job agent:	No
Career info provided:	Yes
Links to other sites:	Yes

SITE'S SELF DESCRIPTION

Cool Works® is about finding a seasonal job or career in some of the greatest places on Earth. We offer thousands of jobs in national and state parks, summer and ski resorts, camps, ranches, adventure travel companies and more. Our 5,700-member social network provides a place to compare and share work and life experiences in these unique places.

Contact Information

Name: Bill Berg
Phone: 406-848-2380   E-Mail: greatjobs@coolworks.com

Coroflot

www.coroflot.com
Core77, Inc.

GENERAL SITE INFORMATION

Date activated online:	1997
Location of site headquarters:	New York, NY
Number of people who visit the site:	821,000 unique visitors/month
Time spent on site:	4:32 minutes/visit

JOB POSTINGS

Post full time jobs:	Yes
Post part time/contract/consulting jobs:	Yes - Free lance, Contract
Most prevalent types of jobs posted:	Creative: Design, Direction, Strategy
Distribution:	International
Number of job postings:	1,000
Top salary levels of jobs:	$50-75K, $76-S00K/yr
Source of postings:	Employers, Staffing

RESUME SERVICES

Are resumes or profiles posted on the site:	Yes
How long can you store:	Indefinitely
Who can post a resume:	Those registered
Fee to post:	None
Confidentiality available:	No

OTHER SERVICES

Is a listserv or discussion forum offered:	No
Are assessment instruments offered:	No
Automated job agent:	Yes
Career info provided:	Yes
Links to other sites:	No

SITE'S SELF DESCRIPTION

Coroflot is an employment and community site focused on the creative industries and creative professionals. Coroflot has a robust job board covering a wide range of creative disciplines while also allowing individuals to promote themselves as a design resource by creating an online profile and portfolio. The site functions as an inspiration source for all creatives.

Contact Information

Name: Coroflot Client Support
Phone: 212-965-1998 x110   E-Mail: support@coroflot.com

Dice.com
www.dice.com
Dice Holdings, Inc.

GENERAL SITE INFORMATION

Date activated online:	1990
Location of site headquarters:	New York, NY
Number of people who visit the site:	2,000,000 unique visitors/month
Time spent on site:	27.0 page views/visitor

JOB POSTINGS

Post full time jobs:	Yes
Post part time/contract/consulting jobs:	Yes - All
Most prevalent types of jobs posted:	Technology
Distribution:	National - USA
Number of job postings:	70,000
Top salary levels of jobs:	$76-100K, $101-150K/yr
Source of postings:	Employers, Staffing

RESUME SERVICES

Are resumes or profiles posted on the site:	Yes
How long can you store:	Indefinitely
Who can post a resume:	Those in the field
Fee to post:	None
Confidentiality available:	Yes

OTHER SERVICES

Is a listserv or discussion forum offered:	Yes
Are assessment instruments offered:	No
Automated job agent:	Yes
Career info provided:	Yes
Links to other sites:	Yes

SITE'S SELF DESCRIPTION

Dice, a Dice Holdings, Inc. service, is the leading career site for technology and engineering professionals. With a 20-year track record of meeting the needs of technology professionals, companies and recruiters, our specialty focus and exposure to highly skilled professional communities enable employers to reach hard-to-find, experienced and qualified candidates.

Contact Information

Name: Dice.com Sales
Phone: 877-386-3323   E-Mail: sales@dice.com

disABLEDperson.com
www.disabledperson.com
disABLEDperson, Inc.

GENERAL SITE INFORMATION

Date activated online:	April, 2002
Location of site headquarters:	Encinitas, CA
Number of people who visit the site:	5,984 unique visitors/month
Time spent on site:	4.2 page views/visitor

JOB POSTINGS

Post full time jobs:	Yes
Post part time/contract/consulting jobs:	No
Most prevalent types of jobs posted:	Wide variety
Distribution:	National - USA
Number of job postings:	7,000
Top salary levels of jobs:	Not Reported
Source of postings:	Employers

RESUME SERVICES

Are resumes or profiles posted on the site:	Yes
How long can you store:	85 days
Who can post a resume:	Those registered
Fee to post:	None
Confidentiality available:	Yes

OTHER SERVICES

Is a listserv or discussion forum offered:	No
Are assessment instruments offered:	No
Automated job agent:	No
Career info provided:	Yes
Links to other sites:	Yes

SITE'S SELF DESCRIPTION

We are a public charity organization whose primary focus is disability employment. We want to help you, a person with a disability find employment. Our portal connects individuals with disabilities with proactive employers. So come, post your resume and look for a job. Its free! Our goal is to get as many jobs for people with disabilities as possible.

Contact Information

Name: Information
Phone: 760-420-1269   E-Mail: info@disabledperson.com

DiversityJobs.com
www.diversityjobs.com
LatPro, Inc.

GENERAL SITE INFORMATION

Date activated online:	2006
Location of site headquarters:	Plantation, FL
Number of people who visit the site:	250,000+ unique visitors/month
Time spent on site:	4:15 minutes/visit

JOB POSTINGS

Post full time jobs:	Yes
Post part time/contract/consulting jobs:	Yes - All
Most prevalent types of jobs posted:	AD, HR, SM, Healthcare
Distribution:	National - USA
Number of job postings:	440,000
Top salary levels of jobs:	Not Reported
Source of postings:	Employers, Other sites

RESUME SERVICES

Are resumes or profiles posted on the site:	No
How long can you store:	N/A
Who can post a resume:	N/A
Fee to post:	N/A
Confidentiality available:	N/A

OTHER SERVICES

Is a listserv or discussion forum offered:	Yes
Are assessment instruments offered:	Yes
Automated job agent:	Yes
Career info provided:	Yes
Links to other sites:	Yes

SITE'S SELF DESCRIPTION

Developed by LatPro, Inc., DiversityJobs.com holds the #1 ranking on Google, Yahoo! and Bing for the search term "diversity jobs." Our mission is to equip African-Americans, women, Hispanics, veterans, persons with disabilities, Asian-Americans, Native Americans, members of the LGBT community and others with current jobs from employers dedicated to a diverse workforce.

Contact Information

Name: Rob Steward
Phone: 954-727-3863   E-Mail: sales@latpro.com

eFinancialCareers.com
www.efinancialcareers.com
Dice Holdings, Inc.

GENERAL SITE INFORMATION

Date activated online: 2000
Location of site headquarters: New York, NY
Number of people who visit the site: 350,000 unique visitors/month
Time spent on site: 10.7 page views/visitor

JOB POSTINGS

Post full time jobs: Yes
Post part time/contract/consulting jobs: Yes - All
Most prevalent types of jobs posted: Financial markets
Distribution: International
Number of job postings: 1,700
Top salary levels of jobs: Up to $250K+/yr
Source of postings: Employers

RESUME SERVICES

Are resumes or profiles posted on the site: Yes
How long can you store: Indefinitely
Who can post a resume: Those in the field
Fee to post: None
Confidentiality available: Yes

OTHER SERVICES

Is a listserv or discussion forum offered: No
Are assessment instruments offered: No
Automated job agent: Yes
Career info provided: Yes
Links to other sites: Yes

SITE'S SELF DESCRIPTION

eFinancialCareers, a Dice Holdings, Inc. service, is the leading global career site network in the investment banking, asset management and securities industries. eFinancialCareers provides job postings, news, salary surveys and career advice; reaches professionals in over 30 financial market sectors; and has a network of 25+ co-branded career sites in the NA industry.

Contact Information

Name: eFinancialCareers Sales
Phone: 800-380-9040   E-Mail: sales@efinancialcareers.com

EHSCareers.com
www.ehscareers.com
EHSCareers.com, Inc.

GENERAL SITE INFORMATION

Date activated online:	2003
Location of site headquarters:	Watkinsville, GA
Number of people who visit the site:	35,458 unique visitors/month
Time spent on site:	5.7 pageviews/visitor

JOB POSTINGS

Post full time jobs:	Yes
Post part time/contract/consulting jobs:	Yes - All
Most prevalent types of jobs posted:	Environment, Safety, Occupational Health
Distribution:	International
Number of job postings:	550+
Top salary levels of jobs:	$151-200K, $201-250K/yr
Source of postings:	Employers, Staffing

RESUME SERVICES

Are resumes or profiles posted on the site:	Yes
How long can you store:	6 months
Who can post a resume:	Those registered
Fee to post:	None
Confidentiality available:	Yes

OTHER SERVICES

Is a listserv or discussion forum offered:	No
Are assessment instruments offered:	No
Automated job agent:	Yes
Career info provided:	Yes
Links to other sites:	Yes

SITE'S SELF DESCRIPTION

EHSCareers.com has been the leading job board for the environmental, occupational health and safety profession since 2003. The site is free to job seekers. Recruiters and employers pay a fee for job postings and access to job seeker profiles. EHSCareers.com is also the official job board for the National Safety Council and the National Association of EHS Managers.

Contact Information

Name: Randy Williams
Phone: 877-213-3377   E-Mail: randywilliams@ehscareers.com

EmployeeBenefitsJobs.com
www.employeebenefitsjobs.com
BenefitsLink.com, Inc.

GENERAL SITE INFORMATION

Date activated online:	December, 1996
Location of site headquarters:	Winter Park, FL
Number of people who visit the site:	16,000 unique visitors/month
Time spent on site:	9:00 minutes/visit

JOB POSTINGS

Post full time jobs:	Yes
Post part time/contract/consulting jobs:	Yes - All
Most prevalent types of jobs posted:	Employee benefits administration
Distribution:	National - USA
Number of job postings:	225
Top salary levels of jobs:	$51-75K, $76-100K/yr
Source of postings:	Employers, Staffing

RESUME SERVICES

Are resumes or profiles posted on the site:	Yes
How long can you store:	2 years
Who can post a resume:	Those in the field
Fee to post:	None
Confidentiality available:	Yes

OTHER SERVICES

Is a listserv or discussion forum offered:	Yes
Are assessment instruments offered:	No
Automated job agent:	Yes
Career info provided:	Yes
Links to other sites:	Yes

SITE'S SELF DESCRIPTION

Online since 1996, EmployeeBenefitsJobs.com has high Google visibility and a loyal audience. A link to each job is published in email newsletters sent to 25,000 subscribers daily by affiliate BenefitsLink.com, the leading and first Web-site for the employee benefits community, where an advertisement for the job board appears on every page.

Contact Information

Name: Mary Hall
Phone: 407-644-4146   E-Mail: maryhall@benefitslink.com

ExecuNet

www.execunet.com
ExecuNet

GENERAL SITE INFORMATION

Location of site headquarters:	Norwalk, CT
Number of people who visit the site:	1,000,000 unique visitors/month
Time spent on site:	4.8 page views/visitor
Date activated online:	1995

JOB POSTINGS

Post full time jobs:	Yes
Post part time/contract/consulting jobs:	Yes - Contract
Most prevalent types of jobs posted:	HR, IS, MG, SM
Distribution:	National - USA
Number of job postings:	2,600+
Top salary levels of jobs:	Up to $600K+/yr
Source of postings:	Employers, Staffing

RESUME SERVICES

Are resumes or profiles posted on the site:	Yes
How long can you store:	1 year
Who can post a resume:	Members only (fee)
Fee to post:	Included in membership
Confidentiality available:	Yes

OTHER SERVICES

Is a listserv or discussion forum offered:	Yes
Are assessment instruments offered:	Yes
Automated job agent:	Yes
Career info provided:	Yes
Links to other sites:	Yes

SITE'S SELF DESCRIPTION

ExecuNet is a private membership network for business leaders who believe that the right connections can produce extraordinary results in their careers and organizations. Since 1988, it has provided members access to confidential six-figure job opportunities, proprietary research and pragmatic advice.

Contact Information

Name: Member Services
Phone: 800-637-3126   E-Mail: member.services@execunet.comm

FINS from The Wall Street Journal

www.fins.com
Dow Jones & Company

GENERAL SITE INFORMATION

Date activated online:	2009
Location of site headquarters:	New York, NY
Number of people who visit the site:	40,000,000+ unique visitors/month
Time spent on site:	2:00 minutes/visit

JOB POSTINGS

Post full time jobs:	Yes
Post part time/contract/consulting jobs:	Yes - All
Most prevalent types of jobs posted:	FA, IS, SM
Distribution:	International
Number of job postings:	11,000+
Top salary levels of jobs:	Up to $500K+/yr
Source of postings:	Employers, Staffing

RESUME SERVICES

Are resumes or profiles posted on the site:	Yes
How long can you store:	Indefinitely
Who can post a resume:	Those registered
Fee to post:	None
Confidentiality available:	Yes

OTHER SERVICES

Is a listserv or discussion forum offered:	Yes
Are assessment instruments offered:	No
Automated job agent:	Yes
Career info provided:	Yes
Links to other sites:	Yes

SITE'S SELF DESCRIPTION

FINS.com from The Wall Street Journal combines great jobs with industry-specific news and advice to help you find jobs, manage your career and get ahead. Our free, targeted sites for finance, technology and sales and marketing professionals help you stay on top of your career, whether you're actively looking for a job or working to excel in your current position.

Contact Information

Name: Sales Inquiries
Phone: 1-877-FINS-450   E-Mail: sales@fins.com

FlexJobs
www.flexjobs.com
FlexJobs Corporation

GENERAL SITE INFORMATION

Date activated online:	June, 2007
Location of site headquarters:	San Francisco, CA
Number of people who visit the site:	80,000 unique visitors/month
Time spent on site:	5:30 minutes/visit

JOB POSTINGS

Post full time jobs:	Yes
Post part time/contract/consulting jobs:	Yes - All
Most prevalent types of jobs posted:	Telecommuting & flexible jobs
Distribution:	International
Number of job postings:	2,000
Top salary levels of jobs:	Up to $100K+/yr
Source of postings:	Employers

RESUME SERVICES

Are resumes or profiles posted on the site:	Yes
How long can you store:	Indefinitely
Who can post a resume:	Those registered
Fee to post:	$49.95/year
Confidentiality available:	Yes

OTHER SERVICES

Is a listserv or discussion forum offered:	No
Are assessment instruments offered:	Yes
Automated job agent:	Yes
Career info provided:	No
Links to other sites:	No

SITE'S SELF DESCRIPTION

FlexJobs is an innovative job site dedicated to bringing legitimate, flexible telecommuting jobs -- and the work-life, economic, and environmental benefits they offer -- to the people who want them. FlexJobs provides job-seekers a way to find qualified, hand-screened jobs quickly, easily, and safely and is a free resource for employers to recruit top-notch candidates.

Contact Information

Name: Sara Sutton Fell
Phone: 866-991-9222   E-Mail: sara@flexjobs.com

GARP Career Center
http://careers.garp.com
Global Association of Risk Professionals (GARP)

GENERAL SITE INFORMATION

Date activated online:	2003
Location of site headquarters:	Jersey City, NJ
Number of people who visit the site:	10,658 unique visitors/month
Time spent on site:	3:12 minutes/visit

JOB POSTINGS

Post full time jobs:	Yes
Post part time/contract/consulting jobs:	No
Most prevalent types of jobs posted:	Banking, Investing, Financial Risk
Distribution:	International
Number of job postings:	100
Top salary levels of jobs:	Up to $250K+/yr
Source of postings:	Employers

RESUME SERVICES

Are resumes or profiles posted on the site:	Yes
How long can you store:	1 year
Who can post a resume:	Those in the field
Fee to post:	None
Confidentiality available:	Yes

OTHER SERVICES

Is a listserv or discussion forum offered:	No
Are assessment instruments offered:	No
Automated job agent:	Yes
Career info provided:	No
Links to other sites:	No

SITE'S SELF DESCRIPTION

The Global Association of Risk Professionals (GARP) is the leading industry association for financial risk management professionals, with over 150,000 members from 195 countries and territories. The GARP Career Center caters to the complexities of financial risk management recruiting. We serve the banking, finance, financial services, consulting and government sectors.

Contact Information

Name: Mary Jo Roberts
Phone: 201-719-7216   E-Mail: maryjo.roberts@garp.com

Great Insurance Jobs
www.greatinsurancejobs.com
Great Insurance Jobs, Inc.

GENERAL SITE INFORMATION

Date activated online:	2001
Location of site headquarters:	Orlando, FL
Number of people who visit the site:	115,000 unique visitors/month
Time spent on site:	3:26 minutes/visit

JOB POSTINGS

Post full time jobs:	Yes
Post part time/contract/consulting jobs:	Yes - All
Most prevalent types of jobs posted:	Insurance-related
Distribution:	USA, Canada
Number of job postings:	3,000
Top salary levels of jobs:	Up to $200K+/yr
Source of postings:	Employers

RESUME SERVICES

Are resumes or profiles posted on the site:	Yes
How long can you store:	Indefinitely
Who can post a resume:	Those in the field
Fee to post:	None
Confidentiality available:	Yes

OTHER SERVICES

Is a listserv or discussion forum offered:	No
Are assessment instruments offered:	No
Automated job agent:	Yes
Career info provided:	Yes
Links to other sites:	Yes

SITE'S SELF DESCRIPTION

Great Insurance Jobs operates the insurance industry's leading career site. Functional products and services create the ultimate solution for a variety of hiring needs. Employers can reach the most qualified candidates by posting jobs or by searching our database of insurance-only professionals.

Contact Information

Name: Heather Deyrieux
Phone: 800-818-4898 x2121   E-Mail: heather@greatinsurancejobs.com

Hcareers
www.hcareers.com
onTargetjobs, Inc.

GENERAL SITE INFORMATION

Date activated online:	1998
Location of site headquarters:	Vancouver, British Columbia, Canada
Number of people who visit the site:	800,000 unique visitors/month
Time spent on site:	7:00 minutes/visit

JOB POSTINGS

Post full time jobs:	Yes
Post part time/contract/consulting jobs:	Yes - All
Most prevalent types of jobs posted:	MG, OP, Hotel, Restaurant
Distribution:	USA, Canada, United Kingdom
Number of job postings:	6,400
Top salary levels of jobs:	$201-250K, $251K+/yr
Source of postings:	Employers

RESUME SERVICES

Are resumes or profiles posted on the site:	Yes
How long can you store:	1 year
Who can post a resume:	Anyone
Fee to post:	None
Confidentiality available:	Yes

OTHER SERVICES

Is a listserv or discussion forum offered:	No
Are assessment instruments offered:	Yes
Automated job agent:	Yes
Career info provided:	Yes
Links to other sites:	Yes

SITE'S SELF DESCRIPTION

Are you looking for a hotel, restaurant, food service, or any other hospitality job? Find your next hospitality career on Hcareers, the leading online job board for the hospitality industry. Hcareers attracts over 800,000 unique job seeker visitors each month — more than any other niche job board. Employers can also review over 160,000 resumes posted by job seekers.

Contact Information

Name: Greg Tareta
Phone: 800.832.3738 x7899   E-Mail: greg.tareta@hcareers.com

HEALTHeCAREERS Network
www.healthecareers.com
onTargetjobs, Inc.

GENERAL SITE INFORMATION

Date activated online:	1999
Location of site headquarters:	Englewood, CO
Number of people who visit the site:	515,000 unique visitors/month
Time spent on site:	5:00 minutes/visit

JOB POSTINGS

Post full time jobs:	Yes
Post part time/contract/consulting jobs:	Yes - All
Most prevalent types of jobs posted:	AD, Healthcare, Physician, Nurse
Distribution:	USA, Canada
Number of job postings:	13,000
Top salary levels of jobs:	$51-75K, $76-100K+/yr
Source of postings:	Employers, Staffing

RESUME SERVICES

Are resumes or profiles posted on the site:	Yes
How long can you store:	Indefinitely
Who can post a resume:	Those in the field
Fee to post:	None
Confidentiality available:	Yes

OTHER SERVICES

Is a listserv or discussion forum offered:	Yes
Are assessment instruments offered:	Yes
Automated job agent:	Yes
Career info provided:	Yes
Links to other sites:	Yes

SITE'S SELF DESCRIPTION

HEALTHeCAREERS Network is a unique recruitment tool made possible through partnerships with more than 70 healthcare associations. The Network gives employers a single point of access to recruit from participating associations and hundreds of partner Web-sites. Services also include online print campaign management and access to association career fairs.

Contact Information

Name: Joe Steiner
Phone: 303-833-7372

E-Mail: joe.steiner@ontargetjobs.com

HealthJobsNationwide.com
www.healthjobsnationwide.com
Healthcare Staffing Innovations, LLC

GENERAL SITE INFORMATION

Date activated online:	April, 2003
Location of site headquarters:	Woodstock, GA
Number of people who visit the site:	155,000 unique visitors/month
Time spent on site:	2:33 minutes/visit

JOB POSTINGS

Post full time jobs:	Yes
Post part time/contract/consulting jobs:	Yes - All
Most prevalent types of jobs posted:	Physician, Nurse, Therapy, Pharmacy
Distribution:	National - USA
Number of job postings:	40,000+
Top salary levels of jobs:	Up to $500K+/yr
Source of postings:	Employers, Staffing

RESUME SERVICES

Are resumes or profiles posted on the site:	Yes
How long can you store:	Indefinitely
Who can post a resume:	Those in the field
Fee to post:	None
Confidentiality available:	Yes

OTHER SERVICES

Is a listserv or discussion forum offered:	No
Are assessment instruments offered:	No
Automated job agent:	Yes
Career info provided:	No
Links to other sites:	Yes

SITE'S SELF DESCRIPTION

HealthJobsNationwide.com powers seven unique brands designed to serve specific segments of the healthcare industry. The seven communities we serve include physicians, advanced practice clinicians, nursing, pharmacy, therapy, technologists and health administration. While we target clinicians individually, our clients post their jobs and search resumes all in one place.

Contact Information

Name: Dustin Martin
Phone: 888-861-5627   E-Mail: info@healthjobsnationwide.com

HigherEdJobs
www.higheredjobs.com
Internet Employment Linkage, Inc.

GENERAL SITE INFORMATION

Date activated online:	1996
Location of site headquarters:	State College, PA
Number of people who visit the site:	780,000 unique visitors/month
Time spent on site:	7.0 page views/visitor

JOB POSTINGS

Post full time jobs:	Yes
Post part time/contract/consulting jobs:	Yes - Part time/Adjunct Faculty
Most prevalent types of jobs posted:	Higher Education (All Departments)
Distribution:	International
Number of job postings:	13,000+
Top salary levels of jobs:	$200-225K/yr
Source of postings:	Employers, Staffing

RESUME SERVICES

Are resumes or profiles posted on the site:	Yes
How long can you store:	Indefinitely
Who can post a resume:	Those registered
Fee to post:	None
Confidentiality available:	Yes

OTHER SERVICES

Is a listserv or discussion forum offered:	No
Are assessment instruments offered:	No
Automated job agent:	Yes
Career info provided:	Yes
Links to other sites:	Yes

SITE'S SELF DESCRIPTION

HigherEdJobs is the leading source for jobs and career information in academia. During 2010, more than 4,200 colleges and universities posted over 79,000 job postings to the company's Web-site. Serving higher education since 1996, HigherEdJobs now receives two million visits a month from 780,000 unique visitors representing both higher education professionals and couples.

Contact Information

Name: John Ikenberry
Phone: 814-861-3080   E-Mail: sales@higheredjobs.com

Hospital Dream Jobs
www.hospitaldreamjobs.com
Healthcare Communications, LLC

GENERAL SITE INFORMATION

Date activated online:	2009
Location of site headquarters:	Seattle, WA
Number of people who visit the site:	133,000 unique visitors/month
Time spent on site:	15.0 page views/visit

JOB POSTINGS

Post full time jobs:	Yes
Post part time/contract/consulting jobs:	Yes - All
Most prevalent types of jobs posted:	MG, Physicians, Nursing, Allied Health
Distribution:	National - USA
Number of job postings:	65,000+
Top salary levels of jobs:	Up to $250K+/yr
Source of postings:	Employers

RESUME SERVICES

Are resumes or profiles posted on the site:	Yes
How long can you store:	6 months
Who can post a resume:	Those registered
Fee to post:	None
Confidentiality available:	Yes

OTHER SERVICES

Is a listserv or discussion forum offered:	Yes
Are assessment instruments offered:	No
Automated job agent:	Yes
Career info provided:	Yes
Links to other sites:	Yes

SITE'S SELF DESCRIPTION

Hospital Dream Jobs is unique in offering 65,000+ healthcare jobs, cutting-edge technology and original in-depth healthcare resources all in one place for healthcare professionals! Our updated services in social media marketing get results through branding, blogs, Twitter, and Facebook. Our team has 20 years of experience in healthcare recruiting and Web-site technology.

Contact Information

Name: Allison Rapaport
Phone: 800-277-8455   E-Mail: arapaport@hospitaldreamjobs.com

Hospital Jobs Online
www.hospitaljobsonline.com
Internet Brands, Inc.

GENERAL SITE INFORMATION

Date activated online:	2001
Location of site headquarters:	El Segundo, CA
Number of people who visit the site:	110,000 unique visitors/month
Time spent on site:	2:00 minutes/visit

JOB POSTINGS

Post full time jobs:	Yes
Post part time/contract/consulting jobs:	Yes - All
Most prevalent types of jobs posted:	Nurses, Physicians, Allied Health
Distribution:	International
Number of job postings:	55,000
Top salary levels of jobs:	Not Reported
Source of postings:	Employers

RESUME SERVICES

Are resumes or profiles posted on the site:	Yes
How long can you store:	Indefinitely
Who can post a resume:	Those registered
Fee to post:	None
Confidentiality available:	Yes

OTHER SERVICES

Is a listserv or discussion forum offered:	No
Are assessment instruments offered:	No
Automated job agent:	Yes
Career info provided:	Yes
Links to other sites:	Yes

SITE'S SELF DESCRIPTION

Hospitaljobsonline.com is the #1 hospital job board and the leader in healthcare career resources for doctors, nurses, allied health, and administration job seekers. Employers receive pre-qualified leads and resumes sent daily, access to the resume database and unlimited job postings via bulk upload.

Contact Information

Name: Sales
Phone: 888-613-8844   E-Mail: hjolsales@internetbrands.com

icrunchdata
www.icrunchdata.com
icrunchdata

GENERAL SITE INFORMATION

Date activated online:	2003
Location of site headquarters:	Frisco, TX
Number of people who visit the site:	165,000 unique visitors/month
Time spent on site:	6.1 page views/visitor

JOB POSTINGS

Post full time jobs:	Yes
Post part time/contract/consulting jobs:	Yes - Contract, Consulting
Most prevalent types of jobs posted:	Data, Analytics, Statistics
Distribution:	National - USA
Number of job postings:	5,000
Top salary levels of jobs:	$151-200K, $201-250K/yr
Source of postings:	Employers, Other sites

RESUME SERVICES

Are resumes or profiles posted on the site:	Yes
How long can you store:	Indefinitely
Who can post a resume:	Those registered
Fee to post:	None
Confidentiality available:	Yes

OTHER SERVICES

Is a listserv or discussion forum offered:	No
Are assessment instruments offered:	No
Automated job agent:	Yes
Career info provided:	Yes
Links to other sites:	Yes

SITE'S SELF DESCRIPTION

Icrunchdata is a community of top professionals in data, analytics, and technology! Whether you are looking to hire talent or promote your brand, we can help you reach your advertising goals.

Contact Information

Name: Todd Nevins
Phone: 214-244-5214   E-Mail: tnevins@icrunchdata.com

IEEE Job Site
www.ieee.org/jobs
Institute of Electrical & Electronics Engineers (IEEE)

GENERAL SITE INFORMATION

Date activated online:	2001
Location of site headquarters:	New York, NY
Number of people who visit the site:	47,000 unique visitors/month
Time spent on site:	7:46 minutes/visit

JOB POSTINGS

Post full time jobs:	Yes
Post part time/contract/consulting jobs:	Yes - Part time
Most prevalent types of jobs posted:	EN, IS, MG, Scientist
Distribution:	International
Number of job postings:	13,910
Top salary levels of jobs:	$101-150K/yr
Source of postings:	Employers, Staffing

RESUME SERVICES

Are resumes or profiles posted on the site:	Yes
How long can you store:	Indefinitely
Who can post a resume:	Members only
Fee to post:	None
Confidentiality available:	Yes

OTHER SERVICES

Is a listserv or discussion forum offered:	No
Are assessment instruments offered:	No
Automated job agent:	Yes
Career info provided:	Yes
Links to other sites:	Yes

SITE'S SELF DESCRIPTION

Use the IEEE Job Site to post jobs, search resumes and pre-screen candidates, all of whom are pre-qualified, highly skilled members of the Institute of Electrical & Electronics Engineers (IEEE). Place banner ads on the site or classified and display advertising in IEEE print publications. Our unique "smart job" technology will find you the best candidates available.

Contact Information

Name: Michael Buryk
Phone: 212-419-7571   E-Mail: m.buryk@ieee.org

iHire.com
www.ihire.com
iHire, LLC

GENERAL SITE INFORMATION

Date activated online:	November, 1999
Location of site headquarters:	Frederick, MD
Number of people who visit the site:	1,700,000 unique visitors/month
Time spent on site:	5.1 page views/visitor

JOB POSTINGS

Post full time jobs:	Yes
Post part time/contract/consulting jobs:	Yes - All
Most prevalent types of jobs posted:	Wide variety
Distribution:	National - USA
Number of job postings:	850,000
Top salary levels of jobs:	$76-100K, $101-150K/yr
Source of postings:	Employers, Staffing

RESUME SERVICES

Are resumes or profiles posted on the site:	Yes
How long can you store:	Indefinitely
Who can post a resume:	Those in the field
Fee to post:	None
Confidentiality available:	Yes

OTHER SERVICES

Is a listserv or discussion forum offered:	No
Are assessment instruments offered:	Yes
Automated job agent:	Yes
Career info provided:	Yes
Links to other sites:	Yes

SITE'S SELF DESCRIPTION

iHire job seekers enjoy access to over 850,000 jobs from over 4,300 sources, as well as personalized, daily job feeds, resume and cover letter assistance, and interview and salary negotiation coaching. iHire's industry-specific focus, money-back guarantee, and resume matching technologies provide employers with a risk-free, effective alternative to conventional job boards.

Contact Information

Name: Heather Gonzales
Phone: 877-798-4854   E-Mail: heather.gonzales@ihire.com

Indeed

www.indeed.com
Indeed

GENERAL SITE INFORMATION

Date activated online:	2004
Location of site headquarters:	Stamford, CT
Number of people who visit the site:	40,000,000+ unique visitors/month
Time spent on site:	13:10 minutes/visit

JOB POSTINGS

Post full time jobs:	Yes
Post part time/contract/consulting jobs:	Yes - All
Most prevalent types of jobs posted:	Wide variety
Distribution:	International
Number of job postings:	1,000,000+
Top salary levels of jobs:	Not Reported
Source of postings:	Employers, Other sites

RESUME SERVICES

Are resumes or profiles posted on the site:	Yes
How long can you store:	N/A
Who can post a resume:	N/A
Fee to post:	N/A
Confidentiality available:	N/A

OTHER SERVICES

Is a listserv or discussion forum offered:	Yes
Are assessment instruments offered:	Yes
Automated job agent:	Yes
Career info provided:	Yes
Links to other sites:	Yes

SITE'S SELF DESCRIPTION

Indeed is the #1 job site worldwide, with over 40 million unique visitors per month from more than 50 countries in 24 languages. Job seekers perform more than 1 billion job searches on Indeed each month. Since 2004, Indeed has given job seekers free access to millions of jobs from thousands of company Web-sites and job boards.

Contact Information

Name: Nolan Farris
Phone: 203-564-2405   E-Mail: nolan@indeed.com

Inside Higher Ed
www.insidehighered.com
Inside Higher Ed

GENERAL SITE INFORMATION

Date activated online:	January, 2005
Location of site headquarters:	Washington, D.C.
Number of people who visit the site:	750,000 unique visitors/month
Time spent on site:	2.0 page views/visitor

JOB POSTINGS

Post full time jobs:	Yes
Post part time/contract/consulting jobs:	Yes - Part-time, Adjunct faculty
Most prevalent types of jobs posted:	Higher Ed Faculty, Staff & Other
Distribution:	International
Number of job postings:	8,000
Top salary levels of jobs:	Up to $200K+/yr
Source of postings:	Employers

RESUME SERVICES

Are resumes or profiles posted on the site:	Yes
How long can you store:	Indefinitely
Who can post a resume:	Those registered
Fee to post:	None
Confidentiality available:	Yes

OTHER SERVICES

Is a listserv or discussion forum offered:	No
Are assessment instruments offered:	No
Automated job agent:	Yes
Career info provided:	Yes
Links to other sites:	Yes

SITE'S SELF DESCRIPTION

Inside Higher Ed is the daily news Web-site for higher education professionals. Featuring breaking news, commentary, career advice, blogs, and thousands of faculty, administrative and executive job postings, more than 750,000 unique readers visit the site each month. Job content is integrated throughout the site, reaching passive candidates with related jobs.

Contact Information

Name: Kathlene Collins
Phone: 202-659-9208 x103   E-Mail: recruit@insidehighered.com

JAMA Career Center®
www.jamacareercenter.com
American Medical Association

GENERAL SITE INFORMATION

Date activated online:	2005
Location of site headquarters:	Chicago, IL
Number of people who visit the site:	13,714 unique visitors/month
Time spent on site:	2:55 minutes/visit

JOB POSTINGS

Post full time jobs:	Yes
Post part time/contract/consulting jobs:	Yes - Locum Tenens & other situations
Most prevalent types of jobs posted:	Physician
Distribution:	International
Number of job postings:	5,454
Top salary levels of jobs:	Up to $999K+/yr
Source of postings:	Employers

RESUME SERVICES

Are resumes or profiles posted on the site:	Yes
How long can you store:	Indefinitely
Who can post a resume:	Those in the field
Fee to post:	None
Confidentiality available:	Yes

OTHER SERVICES

Is a listserv or discussion forum offered:	No
Are assessment instruments offered:	Yes
Automated job agent:	Yes
Career info provided:	Yes
Links to other sites:	Yes

SITE'S SELF DESCRIPTION

JAMA Career Center® is a resource for active and passive physician job seekers. The site presents physician career opportunities, news, and resources relevant to the full spectrum of medical practice. Recruiters will find a range of posting options including multi-job packs, site wrapping, employer profiles, banner ads, and print plus online combos.

Contact Information

Name: Classified Advertising
Phone: 800-262-2260   E-Mail: classifieds@ama-assn.org

Job.com
www.job.com
Job.com, Inc.

GENERAL SITE INFORMATION

Date activated online: 2001
Location of site headquarters: Fredericksburg, VA
Number of people who visit the site: 8,500,000 unique visitors/month
Time spent on site: 4:00 minutes/visit

JOB POSTINGS

Post full time jobs:	Yes
Post part time/contract/consulting jobs:	Yes - All
Most prevalent types of jobs posted:	AD, FA, IS, SM
Distribution:	National - USA
Number of job postings:	500,000
Top salary levels of jobs:	Up to $251K+/yr
Source of postings:	Employers, Staffing

RESUME SERVICES

Are resumes or profiles posted on the site:	Yes
How long can you store:	1 year
Who can post a resume:	Members only
Fee to post:	None
Confidentiality available:	Yes

OTHER SERVICES

Is a listserv or discussion forum offered:	No
Are assessment instruments offered:	Yes
Automated job agent:	Yes
Career info provided:	Yes
Links to other sites:	Yes

SITE'S SELF DESCRIPTION

Job.com is an online full service career portal that ranked as the 4th most visited career site in its category in January, 2009, according to comscore/Media Metrix. Job.com specializes in helping employers and recruiters hire qualified employees, while providing job seekers with a variety of career services to enhance and manage their careers.

Contact Information

Name: Customer Service
Phone: 877-7JOBCOM   E-Mail: hireforless@job.com

JobCircle.com
www.jobcircle.com
Human Capital Solutions, LLC

GENERAL SITE INFORMATION

Date activated online:	1998
Location of site headquarters:	West Chester, PA
Number of people who visit the site:	530,000 unique visitors/month
Time spent on site:	7.0 page views/visitor

JOB POSTINGS

Post full time jobs:	Yes
Post part time/contract/consulting jobs:	Yes - All
Most prevalent types of jobs posted:	FA, IS, MG, Healthcare
Distribution:	Regional/USA - Mid-Atlantic (PA, NJ, DE)
Number of job postings:	120,000
Top salary levels of jobs:	$51-75K, $76-100K/yr
Source of postings:	Employers, Staffing

RESUME SERVICES

Are resumes or profiles posted on the site:	Yes
How long can you store:	Indefinitely
Who can post a resume:	Anyone
Fee to post:	None
Confidentiality available:	Yes

OTHER SERVICES

Is a listserv or discussion forum offered:	No
Are assessment instruments offered:	No
Automated job agent:	Yes
Career info provided:	Yes
Links to other sites:	Yes

SITE'S SELF DESCRIPTION

JobCircle.com has been helping employers connect with job seekers since 1998. We're the largest independently owned job board in the Mid-Atlantic region of the United States. With hundreds of thousands of jobs and 1.2 million+ candidates, our regional site provides recruiters with a fresh, inexpensive, and effective alternative to the highly priced national job boards.

Contact Information

Name: Joseph Stubblebine
Phone: 610-431-2001   E-Mail: joe@jobcircle.com

Jobfox
www.jobfox.com
Jobfox

GENERAL SITE INFORMATION

Date activated online:	2005
Location of site headquarters:	McLean, VA
Number of people who visit the site:	2,000,000 unique visitors/month
Time spent on site:	20:00 minutes/visit

JOB POSTINGS

Post full time jobs:	Yes
Post part time/contract/consulting jobs:	Yes - Part time
Most prevalent types of jobs posted:	Wide variety
Distribution:	National - USA
Number of job postings:	Not Reported
Top salary levels of jobs:	Up to $251K+/yr
Source of postings:	Employers, Other sites

RESUME SERVICES

Are resumes or profiles posted on the site:	Yes
How long can you store:	Indefinitely
Who can post a resume:	Anyone
Fee to post:	None
Confidentiality available:	Yes

OTHER SERVICES

Is a listserv or discussion forum offered:	No
Are assessment instruments offered:	Yes
Automated job agent:	Yes
Career info provided:	Yes
Links to other sites:	Yes

SITE'S SELF DESCRIPTION

Jobfox is the fastest-growing career networking site that connects professionals with recruiters. Jobfox gets candidates in the "inner circle" by creating personal introductions to recruiters at companies of interest. For recruiters, Jobfox Boost(SM) automates the process of building talent pipelines, giving them a high volume, high speed social recruiting solution.

Contact Information

Name: Dan Kimball
Phone: 703-748-0162   E-Mail: customerservice@jobfox.com

Jobing.com
www.jobing.com
Jobing

GENERAL SITE INFORMATION

Date activated online:	2000
Location of site headquarters:	Phoenix, AZ
Number of people who visit the site:	1,500,000 unique visitors/month
Time spent on site:	10:00 minutes/visit

JOB POSTINGS

Post full time jobs:	Yes
Post part time/contract/consulting jobs:	Yes - All
Most prevalent types of jobs posted:	Wide variety
Distribution:	Regional/USA: Multiple states
Number of job postings:	500,000+
Top salary levels of jobs:	Not Reported
Source of postings:	Employers

RESUME SERVICES

Are resumes or profiles posted on the site:	Yes
How long can you store:	Indefinitely
Who can post a resume:	Anyone
Fee to post:	None
Confidentiality available:	Yes

OTHER SERVICES

Is a listserv or discussion forum offered:	Yes
Are assessment instruments offered:	Yes
Automated job agent:	Yes
Career info provided:	Yes
Links to other sites:	Yes

SITE'S SELF DESCRIPTION

A three-time Inc. 500 fastest-growing company, Jobing.com is the nation's largest locally-focused job board community whose mission is to connect local employers and job seekers through a variety of resources such as job postings, resume search, employment branding banners and advertising, event listings and advanced company profiles.

Contact Information

Name: Theresa Maher
Phone: 602-571-0793   E-Mail: theresa.maher@jobing.com

Job Rooster
www.jobrooster.com
Job Rooster

GENERAL SITE INFORMATION

Date activated online:	2009
Location of site headquarters:	San Francisco, CA
Number of people who visit the site:	25,000 unique visitors/month
Time spent on site:	5:25 minutes/visit

JOB POSTINGS

Post full time jobs:	Yes
Post part time/contract/consulting jobs:	Yes - All
Most prevalent types of jobs posted:	Wide variety
Distribution:	National - USA
Number of job postings:	20,000
Top salary levels of jobs:	Up to $150K+/yr
Source of postings:	Employers

RESUME SERVICES

Are resumes or profiles posted on the site:	Yes
How long can you store:	Indefinitely
Who can post a resume:	Anyone
Fee to post:	None
Confidentiality available:	Yes

OTHER SERVICES

Is a listserv or discussion forum offered:	No
Are assessment instruments offered:	No
Automated job agent:	Yes
Career info provided:	Yes
Links to other sites:	No

SITE'S SELF DESCRIPTION

Jobrooster.com allows you to engage any candidate, anytime, anywhere on their mobile phone. We help job seekers in any industry or career field have access to jobs even when they are not in front of a computer. The service is primarily used by enterprise recruiters, third party staffing agencies, and recruitment advertising agencies to recruit smarter, not harder.

Contact Information

Name: Information
Phone: 800-377-9202   E-Mail: info@jobrooster.com

JobsInBenefits.com
www.jobsinbenefits.com
International Foundation of Employee Benefit Plans (IFEBP)

GENERAL SITE INFORMATION

Date activated online:	1998
Location of site headquarters:	Milwaukee, WI
Number of people who visit the site:	80,000 unique visitors/month
Time spent on site:	4:00 minutes/visit

JOB POSTINGS

Post full time jobs:	Yes
Post part time/contract/consulting jobs:	Yes - All
Most prevalent types of jobs posted:	HR, MG, Benefits, Compensation
Distribution:	International
Number of job postings:	150
Top salary levels of jobs:	$76-100K, $151-200K/yr
Source of postings:	Employers, Staffing

RESUME SERVICES

Are resumes or profiles posted on the site:	Yes
How long can you store:	6 months
Who can post a resume:	Those in the field
Fee to post:	IFEBP Members: None
Confidentiality available:	Yes

OTHER SERVICES

Is a listserv or discussion forum offered:	Yes
Are assessment instruments offered:	No
Automated job agent:	No
Career info provided:	Yes
Links to other sites:	No

SITE'S SELF DESCRIPTION

JobsInBenefits.com brings together qualified benefits/HR professionals with the companies that seek them. Because this job site is hosted by a respected association, recruiters can expect to find resumes from highly qualified benefits/HR professionals. Recruiters looking to fill multiple positions can save with the purchase of a Job Pack.

Contact Information

Name: Job Posting Service
Phone: 888-334-3327 x4

E-Mail: jobposting@ifebp.org

JobsInLogistics.com
www.jobsinlogistics.com
JobsInLogistics.com, Inc.

GENERAL SITE INFORMATION

Date activated online:	2000
Location of site headquarters:	North Miami Beach, FL
Number of people who visit the site:	300,000 unique visitors/month
Time spent on site:	7.0 page views/visitor

JOB POSTINGS

Post full time jobs:	Yes
Post part time/contract/consulting jobs:	Yes - All
Most prevalent types of jobs posted:	Logistics, Transportation, Warehousing
Distribution:	USA, Canada
Number of job postings:	6,000
Top salary levels of jobs:	Up to $251K+/yr
Source of postings:	Employers, Staffing

RESUME SERVICES

Are resumes or profiles posted on the site:	Yes
How long can you store:	Indefinitely
Who can post a resume:	Anyone
Fee to post:	None
Confidentiality available:	Yes

OTHER SERVICES

Is a listserv or discussion forum offered:	No
Are assessment instruments offered:	No
Automated job agent:	Yes
Career info provided:	Yes
Links to other sites:	Yes

SITE'S SELF DESCRIPTION

JobsInLogistics.com is North America's largest and most cost effective career and recruiting job board for the logistics, supply chain, manufacturing, transportation, distribution, purchasing, materials management and warehousing professions. JobsInLogistics.com conducts extensive target marketing to attract the top quality candidates in this niche area.

Contact Information

Name: Amy Noah
Phone: 877-562-7678   E-Mail: amy@jobsinlogistics.com

JobsInManufacturing.com
www.jobsinmanufacturing.com
JobsInLogistics.com, Inc.

GENERAL SITE INFORMATION

Date activated online:	2002
Location of site headquarters:	North Miami Beach, FL
Number of people who visit the site:	50,000 unique visitors/month
Time spent on site:	6.0 page views/visitor

JOB POSTINGS

Post full time jobs:	Yes
Post part time/contract/consulting jobs:	Yes - Part time
Most prevalent types of jobs posted:	EN, Manufacturing
Distribution:	USA, Canada
Number of job postings:	1,500
Top salary levels of jobs:	Up to $251K+/yr
Source of postings:	Employers, Staffing

RESUME SERVICES

Are resumes or profiles posted on the site:	Yes
How long can you store:	Indefinitely
Who can post a resume:	Anyone
Fee to post:	None
Confidentiality available:	Yes

OTHER SERVICES

Is a listserv or discussion forum offered:	No
Are assessment instruments offered:	No
Automated job agent:	Yes
Career info provided:	Yes
Links to other sites:	Yes

SITE'S SELF DESCRIPTION

JobsInManufacturing.com is the leading job board for the manufacturing industry. By target marketing the manufacturing industry, we attract the leading professionals in plant management, production planning, materials management, engineering, quality control, purchasing, maintenance and hourly associates.

Contact Information

Name: Amy Noah
Phone: 877-562-7678   E-Mail: amy@jobsinlogistics.com

JobsInME.com
www.jobsinme.com
JobsInTheUS.com

GENERAL SITE INFORMATION

Date activated online:	1999
Location of site headquarters:	Westbrook, ME
Number of people who visit the site:	144,215 unique visitors/month
Time spent on site:	9:00 minutes/visit

JOB POSTINGS

Post full time jobs:	Yes
Post part time/contract/consulting jobs:	Yes - Part time, Contract, Consulting
Most prevalent types of jobs posted:	Wide variety
Distribution:	Regional - Maine
Number of job postings:	5,902
Top salary levels of jobs:	Not Reported
Source of postings:	Employers

RESUME SERVICES

Are resumes or profiles posted on the site:	Yes
How long can you store:	2 years
Who can post a resume:	Those registered
Fee to post:	None
Confidentiality available:	No

OTHER SERVICES

Is a listserv or discussion forum offered:	No
Are assessment instruments offered:	No
Automated job agent:	Yes
Career info provided:	Yes
Links to other sites:	Yes

SITE'S SELF DESCRIPTION

JobsInME.com's mission is to help job seekers find real, local jobs in Maine and reach their career goals. Job seekers can search jobs by location, category, duration and more. All employment opportunities are conveniently organized to facilitate job searching. Job seekers can save their custom search preferences and receive Job Alert emails on a daily/weekly basis.

Contact Information

Name: Information
Phone: 877-374-1088   E-Mail: info@jobsintheus.com

JobsinTrucks.com
www.jobsintrucks.com
JobsinLogistics.com

GENERAL SITE INFORMATION

Date activated online:	2004
Location of site headquarters:	North Miami Beach, FL
Number of people who visit the site:	250,000 unique visitors/month
Time spent on site:	10:00 minutes/visit

JOB POSTINGS

Post full time jobs:	Yes
Post part time/contract/consulting jobs:	Yes - All
Most prevalent types of jobs posted:	Truck Driver
Distribution:	International
Number of job postings:	15,000+
Top salary levels of jobs:	Up to $100K/yr
Source of postings:	Employers

RESUME SERVICES

Are resumes or profiles posted on the site:	Yes
How long can you store:	1 year
Who can post a resume:	In the field
Fee to post:	None
Confidentiality available:	Yes

OTHER SERVICES

Is a listserv or discussion forum offered:	No
Are assessment instruments offered:	No
Automated job agent:	Yes
Career info provided:	Yes
Links to other sites:	Yes

SITE'S SELF DESCRIPTION

JobsInTrucks.com is the #1 driver job board used by employers to hire experienced drivers and owner-operators across the USA and Canada. More than 200,000 drivers visit the site each month to find jobs for Class A and Class B company driver and owner operator positions for long distance, regional and local delivery.

Contact Information

Name: Amy Noah
Phone: 877-562-7678

E-Mail: amy@jobsintrucks.com

JobsRadar
www.jobsradar.com
Percipio Media, LLC

GENERAL SITE INFORMATION

Date activated online:	2009
Location of site headquarters:	Cambridge, MA
Number of people who visit the site:	3,000,000 unique visitors/month
Time spent on site:	2.9 page views/visitor

JOB POSTINGS

Post full time jobs:	Yes
Post part time/contract/consulting jobs:	Yes - All
Most prevalent types of jobs posted:	Wide variety
Distribution:	National - USA
Number of job postings:	1,000,000+
Top salary levels of jobs:	$51-75K, $76-100K/yr
Source of postings:	Employers, Staffing

RESUME SERVICES

Are resumes or profiles posted on the site:	Yes
How long can you store:	Indefinitely
Who can post a resume:	Those registered
Fee to post:	None
Confidentiality available:	Yes

OTHER SERVICES

Is a listserv or discussion forum offered:	No
Are assessment instruments offered:	Yes
Automated job agent:	Yes
Career info provided:	Yes
Links to other sites:	Yes

SITE'S SELF DESCRIPTION

JobsRadar is a one-stop Web-site for job seekers and a user-friendly recruitment resource for HR groups. We not only host resumes but build and host Web-sites for registered users from which they can manage their professional online identity. In addition to job search, career directory, salary discovery, career advancement, education and scholarship tools are available.

Contact Information

Name: Member Services
Phone: 888-671-3118   E-Mail: info@jobsradar.com

JobTarget

www.jobtarget.com
JobTarget

GENERAL SITE INFORMATION

Date activated online:	2001
Location of site headquarters:	New London, CT
Number of people who visit the site:	2,800,000 unique visitors/month
Time spent on site:	3:12 minutes/visit

JOB POSTINGS

Post full time jobs:	Yes
Post part time/contract/consulting jobs:	Yes - All
Most prevalent types of jobs posted:	Wide variety
Distribution:	International
Number of job postings:	460,000
Top salary levels of jobs:	$151-$200K/yr
Source of postings:	Employers, Other sites

RESUME SERVICES

Are resumes or profiles posted on the site:	Yes
How long can you store:	Indefinitely
Who can post a resume:	Anyone
Fee to post:	None
Confidentiality available:	Yes

OTHER SERVICES

Is a listserv or discussion forum offered:	No
Are assessment instruments offered:	No
Automated job agent:	Yes
Career info provided:	Yes
Links to other sites:	Yes

SITE'S SELF DESCRIPTION

More than one thousand organizations, including professional and trade associations, publishers, world-class companies and entrepreneurs, rely on JobTarget's best-in-class technology, generous economics and unmatched service and expertise, to power their career centers. JobTarget also helps employers advertise jobs where they will attract the most qualified talent.

Contact Information

Name: Deborah Katz
Phone: 860-440-0635 x337   E-Mail: d.katz@jobtarget.com

jobWings.com
www.jobwings.com
jobWings.com

GENERAL SITE INFORMATION

Date activated online:	February, 2001
Location of site headquarters:	Montreal, Quebec, Canada
Number of people who visit the site:	53,000+ unique visitors/month
Time spent on site:	1:56 minutes/visit

JOB POSTINGS

Post full time jobs:	Yes
Post part time/contract/consulting jobs:	No
Most prevalent types of jobs posted:	FA, MG
Distribution:	National - Canada
Number of job postings:	90
Top salary levels of jobs:	$51-76K, $76-100K/yr
Source of postings:	Employers

RESUME SERVICES

Are resumes or profiles posted on the site:	No
How long can you store:	N/A
Who can post a resume:	N/A
Fee to post:	N/A
Confidentiality available:	N/A

OTHER SERVICES

Is a listserv or discussion forum offered:	No
Are assessment instruments offered:	No
Automated job agent:	Yes
Career info provided:	Yes
Links to other sites:	Yes

SITE'S SELF DESCRIPTION

jobWings.com is the Internet reference for employment in the fields of finance, accounting and management for intermediate to senior level positions in Canada. Founded in February, 2001, jobWings.com quickly established itself as the leader in that field and remains so today with more than 53,000 visitors per month.

Contact Information

Name: Information
Phone: 888-562-3464

E-Mail: info@publipac.ca

Juju.com

www.juju.com
Juju, Inc.

GENERAL SITE INFORMATION

Date activated online:	2006
Location of site headquarters:	New York, NY
Number of people who visit the site:	2,500,000 unique visitors/month
Time spent on site:	6.7 page views/visitor

JOB POSTINGS

Post full time jobs:	Yes
Post part time/contract/consulting jobs:	Yes - All
Most prevalent types of jobs posted:	Wide variety
Distribution:	National - USA
Number of job postings:	1,000,000+
Top salary levels of jobs:	Not Reported
Source of postings:	Employers, Other sites

RESUME SERVICES

Are resumes or profiles posted on the site:	Yes
How long can you store:	N/A
Who can post a resume:	N/A
Fee to post:	N/A
Confidentiality available:	N/A

OTHER SERVICES

Is a listserv or discussion forum offered:	No
Are assessment instruments offered:	No
Automated job agent:	Yes
Career info provided:	No
Links to other sites:	Yes

SITE'S SELF DESCRIPTION

Juju's goal is to make job search easier. We search jobs found on thousands of employer sites and job boards around the Web and offer features that help you find the one you're looking for more efficiently. We also offer recruitment advertising that allows employers to reach millions of targeted job seekers, enhance their employment brand, and lower their cost-per-hire.

Contact Information

Name: Brendan Cruickshank
Phone: 212-537-3898   E-Mail: sales@juju.com

LatPro

www.latpro.com
LatPro, Inc.

GENERAL SITE INFORMATION

Date activated online:	1997
Location of site headquarters:	Plantation, FL
Number of people who visit the site:	200,000+ unique visitors/month
Time spent on site:	2:52 minutes/visit

JOB POSTINGS

Post full time jobs:	Yes
Post part time/contract/consulting jobs:	Yes - All
Most prevalent types of jobs posted:	EN, FA, SM, Customer Service
Distribution:	International - Latin America
Number of job postings:	15,000
Top salary levels of jobs:	$36-50K, $51-75K/yr
Source of postings:	Employers, Staffing

RESUME SERVICES

Are resumes or profiles posted on the site:	Yes
How long can you store:	Indefinitely
Who can post a resume:	Anyone
Fee to post:	None
Confidentiality available:	Yes

OTHER SERVICES

Is a listserv or discussion forum offered:	Yes
Are assessment instruments offered:	Yes
Automated job agent:	Yes
Career info provided:	Yes
Links to other sites:	Yes

SITE'S SELF DESCRIPTION

Established in 1997, LatPro is the worldwide leader in providing online employment resources for Hispanic and bilingual professionals. With over 330,000 registered candidates and 90 of the Fortune 100 companies using its award-winning service, LatPro.com (available in English, Spanish and Portuguese) is the premier career destination for Latino and bilingual professionals.

Contact Information

Name: Rob Steward
Phone: 954-727-3863   E-Mail: sales@latpro.com

LiveCareer
www.livecareer.com
LiveCareer, Ltd.

GENERAL SITE INFORMATION

Date activated online:	January, 2005
Location of site headquarters:	New York, NY (LiveCareer North America)
Number of people who visit the site:	1,170,000 unique visitors/month
Time spent on site:	6:25 minutes/visit

JOB POSTINGS

Post full time jobs:	No
Post part time/contract/consulting jobs:	No
Most prevalent types of jobs posted:	N/A
Distribution:	N/A
Number of job postings:	N/A
Top salary levels of jobs:	N/A
Source of postings:	N/A

RESUME SERVICES

Are resumes or profiles posted on the site:	Yes
How long can you store:	Indefinitely
Who can post a resume:	Anyone
Fee to post:	None
Confidentiality available:	Yes

OTHER SERVICES

Is a listserv or discussion forum offered:	No
Are assessment instruments offered:	Yes
Automated job agent:	No
Career info provided:	Yes
Links to other sites:	No

SITE'S SELF DESCRIPTION

LiveCareer is the #1 resume building site, according to Comscore. Our Online Resume Builder creates job-winning resumes and cover letters in minutes for all jobs and industries. Our career portal also has free career tests and is integrated with other career sites and companies. Over 11 million people have registered to build a resume, make a career decision or find a job.

Contact Information

Name: Customer Service
Phone: 888-816-0576   E-Mail: customerservice@livecareer.com

Marketing Career Network
www.mcnnetwork.org
Boxwood Technology

GENERAL SITE INFORMATION

Date activated online:	2003
Location of site headquarters:	Hunt Valley, MD
Number of people who visit the site:	25,000 unique visitors/month
Time spent on site:	9:00 minutes/visit

JOB POSTINGS

Post full time jobs:	Yes
Post part time/contract/consulting jobs:	Yes - All
Most prevalent types of jobs posted:	SM, Advertising, Public Relations
Distribution:	International
Number of job postings:	500
Top salary levels of jobs:	$36-50K, $51-75K/yr
Source of postings:	Employers

RESUME SERVICES

Are resumes or profiles posted on the site:	Yes
How long can you store:	1 year
Who can post a resume:	Those in the field
Fee to post:	None
Confidentiality available:	Yes

OTHER SERVICES

Is a listserv or discussion forum offered:	Yes
Are assessment instruments offered:	Yes
Automated job agent:	Yes
Career info provided:	Yes
Links to other sites:	No

SITE'S SELF DESCRIPTION

The Marketing Career Network (MCN) is an online recruitment resource that aligns employers with professional marketing membership organizations. It brings together audiences in every marketing discipline and connects them through a single job board network.

Contact Information

Name: Mary Kay Carey
Phone: 410-891-2402   E-Mail: info@mcnnetwork.org

mediabistro.com
www.mediabistro.com
mediabistro.com

GENERAL SITE INFORMATION

Date activated online:	1997
Location of site headquarters:	New York, NY
Number of people who visit the site:	3,084,995 unique visitors/month
Time spent on site:	2:11 minutes/visit

JOB POSTINGS

Post full time jobs:	Yes
Post part time/contract/consulting jobs:	Yes - Part time
Most prevalent types of jobs posted:	IS, MG, SM, Editorial, Media
Distribution:	International
Number of job postings:	1,300
Top salary levels of jobs:	$76-100K, $151-200K/yr
Source of postings:	Employers, Staffing

RESUME SERVICES

Are resumes or profiles posted on the site:	No
How long can you store:	N/A
Who can post a resume:	N/A
Fee to post:	N/A
Confidentiality available:	N/A

OTHER SERVICES

Is a listserv or discussion forum offered:	Yes
Are assessment instruments offered:	No
Automated job agent:	Yes
Career info provided:	Yes
Links to other sites:	No

SITE'S SELF DESCRIPTION

Mediabistro is the number one destination to reach job seekers in the media industry. Our members/users hear about us through word-of-mouth and at our invitation-only cocktail parties (we don't advertise), so our candidates are savvy, and our traffic is targeted. Post your job online and reach out to over 400,000 registered creative and business-side professionals.

Contact Information

Name: Customer Service
Phone: 212-389-2000   E-Mail: jobcare@mediabistro.com

Meetingjobs
www.meetingjobs.com
Meetingjobs, LLC

GENERAL SITE INFORMATION

Date activated online:	1997
Location of site headquarters:	Southern Pines, NC
Number of people who visit the site:	16,200 unique visitors/month
Time spent on site:	2.2 page views/visitor

JOB POSTINGS

Post full time jobs:	No
Post part time/contract/consulting jobs:	Yes - All
Most prevalent types of jobs posted:	Meeting, Convention, Special events
Distribution:	International
Number of job postings:	40
Top salary levels of jobs:	Up to $220K/yr
Source of postings:	Employers

RESUME SERVICES

Are resumes or profiles posted on the site:	Yes
How long can you store:	Indefinitely
Who can post a resume:	Those in the field
Fee to post:	None
Confidentiality available:	Yes

OTHER SERVICES

Is a listserv or discussion forum offered:	Yes
Are assessment instruments offered:	No
Automated job agent:	Yes
Career info provided:	Yes
Links to other sites:	Yes

SITE'S SELF DESCRIPTION

Meetingjobs, a career job board and Web-site serving the meetings, special events, conference, tradeshow and hospitality industries. The industry's first and most widely used employment site, offering 22,000+ candidates, multiple search options for the hiring official and an up-to-date job board.

Contact Information

Name: Dawn Penfold
Phone: 212-689-7686   E-Mail: dawn@meetingjobs.com

MEP Jobs
www.mepjobs.com
Industry People Group

GENERAL SITE INFORMATION

Date activated online:	1996
Location of site headquarters:	Des Moines, IA
Number of people who visit the site:	50,000 unique visitors/month
Time spent on site:	5:00 minutes/visit

JOB POSTINGS

Post full time jobs:	Yes
Post part time/contract/consulting jobs:	Yes - All
Most prevalent types of jobs posted:	EN, HVAC, Construction
Distribution:	National - USA
Number of job postings:	20,000
Top salary levels of jobs:	$76-100K, $151-200K/yr
Source of postings:	Employers, Staffing

RESUME SERVICES

Are resumes or profiles posted on the site:	Yes
How long can you store:	1 year
Who can post a resume:	Anyone
Fee to post:	None
Confidentiality available:	Yes

OTHER SERVICES

Is a listserv or discussion forum offered:	No
Are assessment instruments offered:	No
Automated job agent:	Yes
Career info provided:	Yes
Links to other sites:	Yes

SITE'S SELF DESCRIPTION

MEP Jobs is the leading career site for the mechanical, electrical and plumbing industries. Each day, thousands of HVAC, facilities, electrical and plumbing professionals and employers find each other on MEP Jobs.

Contact Information

Name: Doug Mitchell
Phone: 888-482-2562   E-Mail: dmitchell@mepjobs.com

MilitaryConnection.com

www.militaryconnection.com
MilitaryConnection.com

GENERAL SITE INFORMATION

Date activated online:	2006
Location of site headquarters:	Simi Valley, CA
Number of people who visit the site:	250,000 unique visitors/month
Time spent on site:	25:00 minutes/visit

JOB POSTINGS

Post full time jobs:	Yes
Post part time/contract/consulting jobs:	Yes - All
Most prevalent types of jobs posted:	Wide variety
Distribution:	International
Number of job postings:	10,000
Top salary levels of jobs:	Up to $251K+/yr
Source of postings:	Employers

RESUME SERVICES

Are resumes or profiles posted on the site:	Yes
How long can you store:	1 year
Who can post a resume:	Those registered
Fee to post:	None
Confidentiality available:	Yes

OTHER SERVICES

Is a listserv or discussion forum offered:	Yes
Are assessment instruments offered:	Yes
Automated job agent:	No
Career info provided:	Yes
Links to other sites:	Yes

SITE'S SELF DESCRIPTION

We are called the Go To Site for jobs, resources, articles and more for military veterans and their families. We offer clients the opportunity to repeat their message in additional and creative ways. We are excellent at reaching passive job seekers too. Users average 25 minutes on site according to Alexa, drawn by the most up-to-date resources and databases for transition.

Contact Information

Name: Debbie Gregory
Phone: 800-817-3777   E-Mail: debbieg@militaryconnection.com

MilitaryHire.com
www.militaryhire.com
The Mentor Group, Inc.

GENERAL SITE INFORMATION

Date activated online:	1999
Location of site headquarters:	The Villages, FL
Number of people who visit the site:	12,000 unique visitors/month
Time spent on site:	1.7 page views/visitor

JOB POSTINGS

Post full time jobs:	Yes
Post part time/contract/consulting jobs:	Yes - All
Most prevalent types of jobs posted:	IS, Defense, Security Clearance
Distribution:	International
Number of job postings:	22,430
Top salary levels of jobs:	$76-100K, $151-200K/yr
Source of postings:	Employers, Other sites

RESUME SERVICES

Are resumes or profiles posted on the site:	Yes
How long can you store:	1 year
Who can post a resume:	Those in the field
Fee to post:	None
Confidentiality available:	Yes

OTHER SERVICES

Is a listserv or discussion forum offered:	Yes
Are assessment instruments offered:	Yes
Automated job agent:	Yes
Career info provided:	Yes
Links to other sites:	Yes

SITE'S SELF DESCRIPTION

MilitaryHire.com is the leading Internet job board for military personnel. As of 2011, we represent nearly 500,000 military candidates. MilitaryHire.com was developed by veterans, for veterans! We specialize in the military experienced candidate. The departing military candidate has the skills that are crucial in today's competitive business environments.

Contact Information

Name: Michael Weiss
Phone: 800-585-3690   E-Mail: mweiss@militaryhire.com

MinnesotaJobs.com
www.minnesotajobs.com
Trumor, Inc.

GENERAL SITE INFORMATION

Date activated online:	1995
Location of site headquarters:	East Bethel, MN
Number of people who visit the site:	100,000+ unique visitors/month
Time spent on site:	6:00+ minutes/visit

JOB POSTINGS

Post full time jobs:	Yes
Post part time/contract/consulting jobs:	Yes - All
Most prevalent types of jobs posted:	EN, FA, IS, Customer Service
Distribution:	Regional/USA: MN
Number of job postings:	2,200
Top salary levels of jobs:	$76-100K, $151-200K/yr
Source of postings:	Employers

RESUME SERVICES

Are resumes or profiles posted on the site:	Yes
How long can you store:	6 months
Who can post a resume:	Those registered
Fee to post:	None
Confidentiality available:	Yes

OTHER SERVICES

Is a listserv or discussion forum offered:	Yes
Are assessment instruments offered:	Yes
Automated job agent:	Yes
Career info provided:	Yes
Links to other sites:	Yes

SITE'S SELF DESCRIPTION

MinnesotaJobs.com is the leading online recruitment resource for Minnesota. In addition to our popular Web-site, celebrating 16 years of helping people, MinnesotaJobs.com has embraced social media outlets to help employers reach highly qualified, achievement oriented future employees.

Contact Information

Name: Penny Freymiller
Phone: 763-784-9393   E-Mail: penny@minnesotajobs.com

Monster.com
www.monster.com
Monster Worldwide, Inc.

GENERAL SITE INFORMATION

Date activated online:	1994
Location of site headquarters:	New York, NY
Number of people who visit the site:	46,000,000 unique visitors/month
Time spent on site:	18.0 page views/visitor

JOB POSTINGS

Post full time jobs:	Yes
Post part time/contract/consulting jobs:	Yes - All
Most prevalent types of jobs posted:	Wide variety
Distribution:	International
Number of job postings:	1,210,000+
Top salary levels of jobs:	Not Reported
Source of postings:	Employers

RESUME SERVICES

Are resumes or profiles posted on the site:	Yes
How long can you store:	2 years
Who can post a resume:	Anyone
Fee to post:	None
Confidentiality available:	Yes

OTHER SERVICES

Is a listserv or discussion forum offered:	Yes
Are assessment instruments offered:	Yes
Automated job agent:	Yes
Career info provided:	Yes
Links to other sites:	Yes

SITE'S SELF DESCRIPTION

Monster.com®, the leading job matching engine, is dedicated to matching talent to opportunity with unrivaled precision. Monster offers employers a full array of online products and services for building and growing a talented workforce and matches seekers to meaningful careers, inspiring them to improve their lives through the world of work.

Contact Information

Name: Monster Customer Central
Phone: 800-MONSTER   E-Mail: moreinfo@monster.com

NACElink Network
www.nacelink.com
The National Association of Colleges & Employers (NACE)

GENERAL SITE INFORMATION

Date activated online:	September, 2002
Location of site headquarters:	Bethlehem, PA
Number of people who visit the site:	2,310,000 unique visitors/month
Time spent on site:	68.7 page views/visitor

JOB POSTINGS

Post full time jobs:	Yes
Post part time/contract/consulting jobs:	Yes - All
Most prevalent types of jobs posted:	Wide variety
Distribution:	National - USA (college students/alumni)
Number of job postings:	704,000 (network-wide)
Top salary levels of jobs:	$35-50K, $51-75K/yr
Source of postings:	Employers

RESUME SERVICES

Are resumes or profiles posted on the site:	Yes
How long can you store:	Indefinitely
Who can post a resume:	Students/alumni
Fee to post:	None
Confidentiality available:	Yes

OTHER SERVICES

Is a listserv or discussion forum offered:	No
Are assessment instruments offered:	No
Automated job agent:	Yes
Career info provided:	No
Links to other sites:	Yes

SITE'S SELF DESCRIPTION

The NACElink Network is a national recruiting network and suite of Web-based recruiting and career services automation tools serving colleges, employers and student/alumni job candidates. The NACElink Network is committed not only to excellence in its products and services but also to focusing on the career center as the provider of jobs and connections to employers.

Contact Information

Name: Sales
Phone: 703-351-0200   E-Mail: sales@nacelink.com

National Healthcare Career Network

www.nhcnnetwork.org
Boxwood Technology

GENERAL SITE INFORMATION

Date activated online:	October, 2007
Location of site headquarters:	Hunt Valley, MD
Number of people who visit the site:	25,116 unique visitors/month
Time spent on site:	9:06 minutes/visit

JOB POSTINGS

Post full time jobs:	Yes
Post part time/contract/consulting jobs:	Yes - All
Most prevalent types of jobs posted:	Nurse, Physician, Allied Health
Distribution:	National - USA
Number of job postings:	2,000+
Top salary levels of jobs:	$76-100K, $101-150K/yr
Source of postings:	Employers

RESUME SERVICES

Are resumes or profiles posted on the site:	Yes
How long can you store:	1 year
Who can post a resume:	Those registered
Fee to post:	None
Confidentiality available:	Yes

OTHER SERVICES

Is a listserv or discussion forum offered:	Yes
Are assessment instruments offered:	Yes
Automated job agent:	Yes
Career info provided:	Yes
Links to other sites:	Yes

SITE'S SELF DESCRIPTION

The National Healthcare Career Network is the fastest growing healthcare association job board network available. The Network links job boards of more than 200 leading healthcare associations, which are the preferred resource for healthcare talent. We can serve employers in filling positions ranging from volunteers and hourly staff to physicians and executive management.

Contact Information

Name: Information
Phone: 888-271-6426   E-Mail: info@hncnnetwork.org

NationJob.com
www.nationjob.com
NationJob Network, Inc.

GENERAL SITE INFORMATION

Date activated online: 1995
Location of site headquarters: Des Moines, IA
Number of people who visit the site: 400,000 unique visitors/month
Time spent on site: 6:30 minutes/visit

JOB POSTINGS

Post full time jobs: Yes
Post part time/contract/consulting jobs: Yes - All
Most prevalent types of jobs posted: Wide variety
Distribution: International
Number of job postings: 60-65,000
Top salary levels of jobs: $51-75K, $76-100K+/yr
Source of postings: Employers

RESUME SERVICES

Are resumes or profiles posted on the site: Yes
How long can you store: Indefinitely
Who can post a resume: Anyone
Fee to post: None
Confidentiality available: Yes

OTHER SERVICES

Is a listserv or discussion forum offered: No
Are assessment instruments offered: Yes
Automated job agent: Yes
Career info provided: Yes
Links to other sites: Yes

SITE'S SELF DESCRIPTION

NationJob.com is the leading provider of community based recruitment. Our core business is our Community Job Network, a partnership between NationJob.com and membership-based organizations offering members significant discounts and creating a custom job site for member employers.

Contact Information

Name: Barb Avery
Phone: 888-256-0920   E-Mail: bavery@nationjob.com

NBMBAA Employment Network
www.nbmbaa.org
National Black MBA Association (NBMBAA)

GENERAL SITE INFORMATION

Date activated online:	1996
Location of site headquarters:	Chicago, IL
Number of people who visit the site:	65,000 unique visitors/month
Time spent on site:	7.0 page views/visitor

JOB POSTINGS

Post full time jobs:	Yes
Post part time/contract/consulting jobs:	Yes - All
Most prevalent types of jobs posted:	FA, MG, OP
Distribution:	National - USA
Number of job postings:	2,000
Top salary levels of jobs:	Up to $250K/yr
Source of postings:	Employers

RESUME SERVICES

Are resumes or profiles posted on the site:	Yes
How long can you store:	5 years
Who can post a resume:	Those registered
Fee to post:	None
Confidentiality available:	Yes

OTHER SERVICES

Is a listserv or discussion forum offered:	No
Are assessment instruments offered:	No
Automated job agent:	Yes
Career info provided:	Yes
Links to other sites:	Yes

SITE'S SELF DESCRIPTION

The National Black MBA Association has and will continue to celebrate the triumphs of the "Black Business Professional" year round. The NBMBAA Employment Network links employers with NBMBAA members, diverse MBA holders and other job seekers.

Contact Information

Name: Sales
Phone: 973-992-7311   E-Mail: nbmbaa-sales@workplacediversity.com

Net-Temps

www.net-temps.com
Net-Temps, Inc.

GENERAL SITE INFORMATION

Date activated online:	1996
Location of site headquarters:	North Chelmsford, MA
Number of people who visit the site:	813,552 unique visitors/month
Time spent on site:	4.8 page views/visitor

JOB POSTINGS

Post full time jobs:	Yes
Post part time/contract/consulting jobs:	Yes - All
Most prevalent types of jobs posted:	AD, FA, IS, MG, Retail
Distribution:	USA, Canada
Number of job postings:	30,695
Top salary levels of jobs:	$50-95K/yr
Source of postings:	Staffing

RESUME SERVICES

Are resumes or profiles posted on the site:	Yes
How long can you store:	Indefinitely
Who can post a resume:	Those registered
Fee to post:	None
Confidentiality available:	Yes

OTHER SERVICES

Is a listserv or discussion forum offered:	Yes
Are assessment instruments offered:	Yes
Automated job agent:	Yes
Career info provided:	Yes
Links to other sites:	Yes

SITE'S SELF DESCRIPTION

Net-Temps is an online job board for temp, temp-to-perm, and direct-hire employment exclusively through staffing companies. Our Job Distribution Network of over 20,000 employment-related Web-sites is one of the most cost-effective approaches to talent acquisition on the Internet. Net-Temps is a top-ranked job board and has over 15 years experience in operation.

Contact Information

Name: Jean Vosler
Phone: 978-251-7272   E-Mail: jean@net-temps.com

NursingJobs.org

www.nursingjobs.org
Internet Brands, Inc.

GENERAL SITE INFORMATION

Date activated online:	2006
Location of site headquarters:	El Segundo, CA
Number of people who visit the site:	200,000 unique visitors/month
Time spent on site:	4:00 minutes/visit

JOB POSTINGS

Post full time jobs:	Yes
Post part time/contract/consulting jobs:	Yes - All
Most prevalent types of jobs posted:	Nurses
Distribution:	International
Number of job postings:	1,000
Top salary levels of jobs:	Not Reported
Source of postings:	Employers

RESUME SERVICES

Are resumes or profiles posted on the site:	Yes
How long can you store:	Indefinitely
Who can post a resume:	Those registered
Fee to post:	None
Confidentiality available:	Yes

OTHER SERVICES

Is a listserv or discussion forum offered:	Yes
Are assessment instruments offered:	No
Automated job agent:	Yes
Career info provided:	Yes
Links to other sites:	Yes

SITE'S SELF DESCRIPTION

With its #1 position on Google and Yahoo! for such terms as "nursing jobs," NursingJobs.org is the Internet's leading site dedicated solely to nurses seeking employment. Advertising to this audience is an ideal way to promote your products, services or organization. We have multiple ad positions available and would welcome the opportunity to work with you.

Contact Information

Name: Sales
Phone: 888-613-8844   E-Mail: sales@nursingjobs.org

Opportunity Knocks
www.opportunityknocks.org
Opportunity Knocks

GENERAL SITE INFORMATION

Date activated online:	1999
Location of site headquarters:	Atlanta, GA
Number of people who visit the site:	288,000 unique visitors/month
Time spent on site:	7:00 minutes/visit

JOB POSTINGS

Post full time jobs:	Yes
Post part time/contract/consulting jobs:	Yes - Part time, Contract, Consulting
Most prevalent types of jobs posted:	Nonprofit
Distribution:	National - USA
Number of job postings:	750
Top salary levels of jobs:	$76-100K/yr
Source of postings:	Employers, Staffing

RESUME SERVICES

Are resumes or profiles posted on the site:	Yes
How long can you store:	Indefinitely
Who can post a resume:	Anyone
Fee to post:	None
Confidentiality available:	Yes

OTHER SERVICES

Is a listserv or discussion forum offered:	Yes
Are assessment instruments offered:	Yes
Automated job agent:	Yes
Career info provided:	Yes
Links to other sites:	Yes

SITE'S SELF DESCRIPTION

Opportunity Knocks is the national online job site focused exclusively on the nonprofit community. We are the premier destination to find nonprofit jobs and access valuable resources for developing successful careers in the nonprofit community. For employers, we are the best way to find qualified candidates and receive valuable information that organizations need.

Contact Information

Name: Joe Folan
Phone: 678-916-3013   E-Mail: jfolan@opportunityknocks.org

PedJobs

www.pedjobs.org
American Academy of Pediatrics

GENERAL SITE INFORMATION

Date activated online:	June, 2001
Location of site headquarters:	Elk Grove Village, IL
Number of people who visit the site:	32,000 unique visitors/month
Time spent on site:	3.2 page views/visitor

JOB POSTINGS

Post full time jobs:	Yes
Post part time/contract/consulting jobs:	Yes - Locum Tenens
Most prevalent types of jobs posted:	Pediatricians, Pediatric nurses
Distribution:	International
Number of job postings:	410
Top salary levels of jobs:	Not Reported
Source of postings:	Employers

RESUME SERVICES

Are resumes or profiles posted on the site:	Yes
How long can you store:	1 year
Who can post a resume:	Those registered
Fee to post:	None
Confidentiality available:	Yes

OTHER SERVICES

Is a listserv or discussion forum offered:	No
Are assessment instruments offered:	Yes
Automated job agent:	Yes
Career info provided:	Yes
Links to other sites:	Yes

SITE'S SELF DESCRIPTION

PedJobs is the official American Academy of Pediatrics resource for pediatric careers. It is the only resource dedicated exclusively to the field of pediatrics and its subspecialties. It is a member of the National Healthcare Career Network (NHCN). PedJobs delivers more pediatric professionals as candidates – and more qualified ones – than any other site in the world.

Contact Information

Name: Mary Lynn Bower
Phone: 847-434-7902   E-Mail: mbower@aap.org

Physics Today Jobs
www.physicstoday.org/jobs
American Institute of Physics (AIP)

GENERAL SITE INFORMATION

Date activated online:	1993
Location of site headquarters:	College Park, MD
Number of people who visit the site:	85,000 unique visitors/month
Time spent on site:	3.8 page views/visitor

JOB POSTINGS

Post full time jobs:	Yes
Post part time/contract/consulting jobs:	Yes - All
Most prevalent types of jobs posted:	EN, Science, Computing
Distribution:	International
Number of job postings:	250
Top salary levels of jobs:	Not Reported
Source of postings:	Employers

RESUME SERVICES

Are resumes or profiles posted on the site:	Yes
How long can you store:	1 year
Who can post a resume:	Those in the field
Fee to post:	None
Confidentiality available:	Yes

OTHER SERVICES

Is a listserv or discussion forum offered:	No
Are assessment instruments offered:	No
Automated job agent:	Yes
Career info provided:	Yes
Links to other sites:	Yes

SITE'S SELF DESCRIPTION

Physics Today Jobs is part of the AIP Career Network. Network partners include the American Association of Physicists in Medicine, American Association of Physics Teachers, American Physical Society, AVS Science and Technology, IEEE Computer Society, and the Society of Physics Students and Sigma Pi Sigma.

Contact Information

Name: Bonnie Feldman
Phone: 301-209-3190   E-Mail: ptjobs@aip.org

PRSA Jobcenter

www.prsa.org/jobcenter
The Public Relations Society of America (PRSA)

GENERAL SITE INFORMATION

Date activated online:	April, 2008
Location of site headquarters:	New York, NY
Number of people who visit the site:	22,580 unique visitors/month
Time spent on site:	2:51 minutes/visit

JOB POSTINGS

Post full time jobs:	Yes
Post part time/contract/consulting jobs:	Yes - All
Most prevalent types of jobs posted:	Public Relations, Corp Communications
Distribution:	National - USA
Number of job postings:	2,200
Top salary levels of jobs:	$151-200K/yr
Source of postings:	Employers, Staffing

RESUME SERVICES

Are resumes or profiles posted on the site:	Yes
How long can you store:	Indefinitely
Who can post a resume:	Anyone
Fee to post:	None
Confidentiality available:	Yes

OTHER SERVICES

Is a listserv or discussion forum offered:	Yes
Are assessment instruments offered:	Yes
Automated job agent:	Yes
Career info provided:	Yes
Links to other sites:	Yes

SITE'S SELF DESCRIPTION

The PRSA Public Relations and Communications Jobcenter is the most targeted community of public relations and communications jobs. Post a job of any length for a discounted flat fee. Whether you are posting PR jobs, community relations, corporate communications, or similar positons, PRSA Jobcenter connects you with more than 77,000 potential employees.

Contact Information

Name: Richard Spector
Phone: 212-460-1406

E-Mail: richard.spector@prsa.org

RegionalHelpWanted.com

www.regionalhelpwanted.com
onTargetjobs, Inc.

GENERAL SITE INFORMATION

Date activated online:	1999
Location of site headquarters:	Denver, CO
Number of people who visit the site:	1,330,000 unique visitors/month
Time spent on site:	8:00 minutes/visit

JOB POSTINGS

Post full time jobs:	Yes
Post part time/contract/consulting jobs:	Yes - All
Most prevalent types of jobs posted:	Wide variety
Distribution:	Local markets in USA, Canada
Number of job postings:	50,000+
Top salary levels of jobs:	$20-30K, $31-50K/yr
Source of postings:	Employers

RESUME SERVICES

Are resumes or profiles posted on the site:	Yes
How long can you store:	Indefinitely
Who can post a resume:	Anyone
Fee to post:	None
Confidentiality available:	Yes

OTHER SERVICES

Is a listserv or discussion forum offered:	No
Are assessment instruments offered:	No
Automated job agent:	Yes
Career info provided:	Yes
Links to other sites:	Yes

SITE'S SELF DESCRIPTION

RegionalHelpWanted.com partners with local broadcast radio stations to design, build and maintain recruitment Web-sites throughout the United States and Canada. RegionalHelpWanted operates over 400 regional sites.

Contact Information

Name: Tony Garcia
Phone: 303-847-4260

E-Mail: tony.garcia@regionalhelpwanted.com

RetirementJobs.com

www.retirementjobs.com
RetirementJobs.com, Inc.

GENERAL SITE INFORMATION

Date activated online:	2006
Location of site headquarters:	Watham, MA
Number of people who visit the site:	250,000 unique visitors/month
Time spent on site:	3:51 minutes/visit

JOB POSTINGS

Post full time jobs:	Yes
Post part time/contract/consulting jobs:	Yes - Part time
Most prevalent types of jobs posted:	SM, Customer Service
Distribution:	National - USA
Number of job postings:	25,000
Top salary levels of jobs:	$36-50K, $51-75K/yr
Source of postings:	Employers, Staffing

RESUME SERVICES

Are resumes or profiles posted on the site:	Yes
How long can you store:	1 year
Who can post a resume:	Those registered
Fee to post:	None
Confidentiality available:	Yes

OTHER SERVICES

Is a listserv or discussion forum offered:	No
Are assessment instruments offered:	No
Automated job agent:	Yes
Career info provided:	Yes
Links to other sites:	Yes

SITE'S SELF DESCRIPTION

RetirementJobs.com is a career portal for Baby Boomers. Its mission is to deliver opportunity, inspiration, community and counsel to people over age 50 seeking work that matches their lifestyle needs. The site is free for job seekers. It makes money by charging placement fees to employers and advertisers.

Contact Information

Name: Pete Mullen
Phone: 781-890-5050   E-Mail: support@retirementjobs.com

Sales Gravy
www.salesgravy.com
3 Palms Publishing Group, LLC

GENERAL SITE INFORMATION

Date activated online:	November, 2006
Location of site headquarters:	Thomson, GA
Number of people who visit the site:	337,210 unique visitors/month
Time spent on site:	10.5 page views/visitor

JOB POSTINGS

Post full time jobs:	Yes
Post part time/contract/consulting jobs:	No
Most prevalent types of jobs posted:	MG, SM, Customer Service
Distribution:	International
Number of job postings:	90,000
Top salary levels of jobs:	$76-100K, $101-150K/yr
Source of postings:	Employers, Staffing

RESUME SERVICES

Are resumes or profiles posted on the site:	Yes
How long can you store:	180 days
Who can post a resume:	Anyone
Fee to post:	None
Confidentiality available:	Yes

OTHER SERVICES

Is a listserv or discussion forum offered:	Yes
Are assessment instruments offered:	Yes
Automated job agent:	Yes
Career info provided:	Yes
Links to other sites:	Yes

SITE'S SELF DESCRIPTION

Sales Gravy is the most visited sales employment Web-site on the planet. Our singular mission is advancing sales as a profession, and we believe that sales professionals are the elite athletes of the business world. On Sales Gravy, we offer thousands of pages of free training and personal development content and host an active community of sales professionals.

Contact Information

Name: Get Help
Phone: 706-664-0810   E-Mail: gethelp@salesgravy.com

Security Jobs Network™
www.securityjobs.net
Security Jobs Network, Inc.

GENERAL SITE INFORMATION

Date activated online:	1998
Location of site headquarters:	Warrenton, VA
Number of people who visit the site:	21,500 unique visitors/month
Time spent on site:	7:00 minutes/visit

JOB POSTINGS

Post full time jobs:	Yes
Post part time/contract/consulting jobs:	No
Most prevalent types of jobs posted:	Individual & Corporate Security
Distribution:	International
Number of job postings:	400
Top salary levels of jobs:	Up to $550K/yr
Source of postings:	Employers, Staffing

RESUME SERVICES

Are resumes or profiles posted on the site:	No
How long can you store:	N/A
Who can post a resume:	N/A
Fee to post:	N/A
Confidentiality available:	N/A

OTHER SERVICES

Is a listserv or discussion forum offered:	No
Are assessment instruments offered:	No
Automated job agent:	No
Career info provided:	No
Links to other sites:	Yes

SITE'S SELF DESCRIPTION

Security Jobs Network™ is a subscription-based service providing up-to-date information based on comprehensive research and the collection of current executive, professional-level security and asset protection opportunities, including corporate security and loss prevention; public, private, civil or criminal investigation; executive protection and other similar positions.

Contact Information

Name: Inquiry
Phone: 866-767-5627   E-Mail: inquiry@securityjobs.net

SHRM HRJobs
www.shrm.org/jobs
Society for Human Resource Management (SHRM)

GENERAL SITE INFORMATION

Date activated online:	1999
Location of site headquarters:	Alexandria, VA
Number of people who visit the site:	116,300 unique visitors/month
Time spent on site:	15:00 minutes/visit

JOB POSTINGS

Post full time jobs:	Yes
Post part time/contract/consulting jobs:	Yes - All
Most prevalent types of jobs posted:	HR
Distribution:	International
Number of job postings:	600
Top salary levels of jobs:	$201-250K, $251K+/yr
Source of postings:	Employers, Staffing

RESUME SERVICES

Are resumes or profiles posted on the site:	Yes
How long can you store:	Indefinitely
Who can post a resume:	Those in the field
Fee to post:	None
Confidentiality available:	Yes

OTHER SERVICES

Is a listserv or discussion forum offered:	No
Are assessment instruments offered:	No
Automated job agent:	Yes
Career info provided:	Yes
Links to other sites:	No

SITE'S SELF DESCRIPTION

The Society for Human Resource Management (SHRM) is the world's largest professional association devoted to human resource management. Our mission is to serve the needs of HR professionals by providing the most current and comprehensive resources, and to advance the profession by promoting HR's essential strategic role.

Contact Information

Name: Omar Scott
Phone: 703-535-6166   E-Mail: omar.scott@shrm.org

Simply Hired

www.simplyhired.com
Simply Hired, Inc.

GENERAL SITE INFORMATION

Date activated online:	2005
Location of site headquarters:	Mountain View, CA
Number of people who visit the site:	14,000,000 unique visitors/month
Time spent on site:	4:00 minutes/visit

JOB POSTINGS

Post full time jobs:	Yes
Post part time/contract/consulting jobs:	Yes - All
Most prevalent types of jobs posted:	Healthcare, Technology
Distribution:	International
Number of job postings:	7,000,000
Top salary levels of jobs:	Not Reported
Source of postings:	Other sites

RESUME SERVICES

Are resumes or profiles posted on the site:	No
How long can you store:	N/A
Who can post a resume:	N/A
Fee to post:	N/A
Confidentiality available:	N/A

OTHER SERVICES

Is a listserv or discussion forum offered:	Yes
Are assessment instruments offered:	Yes
Automated job agent:	Yes
Career info provided:	Yes
Links to other sites:	Yes

SITE'S SELF DESCRIPTION

With more than seven million job listings worldwide, Simply Hired is the world's largest job search engine and recruitment advertising network. The company powers jobs on over 10,000 network partner sites, and operates global sites in 22 countries and 11 languages on six continents.

Contact Information

Name: Matt Baum - Sales
Phone: 650-930-1000   E-Mail: info@simplyhired.com

6FigureJobs.com
http://www.6figurejobs.com
Workstream, Inc.

GENERAL SITE INFORMATION

Date activated online:	1996
Location of site headquarters:	Stamford, CT
Number of people who visit the site:	156,404 unique visitors/month
Time spent on site:	3:31 minutes/visit

JOB POSTINGS

Post full time jobs:	Yes
Post part time/contract/consulting jobs:	Yes - All
Most prevalent types of jobs posted:	FA, IS, MG, SM
Distribution:	International
Number of job postings:	2,700+
Top salary levels of jobs:	Up to $350K+/yr
Source of postings:	Employers, Staffing

RESUME SERVICES

Are resumes or profiles posted on the site:	Yes
How long can you store:	Indefinitely
Who can post a resume:	Those registered
Fee to post:	None
Confidentiality available:	Yes

OTHER SERVICES

Is a listserv or discussion forum offered:	Yes
Are assessment instruments offered:	Yes
Automated job agent:	Yes
Career info provided:	Yes
Links to other sites:	Yes

SITE'S SELF DESCRIPTION

Find and hire today's best executive and senior-level talent. 6FigureJobs.com offers the largest active and passive recruitment database of "pre-screened" executives and senior-level professionals. 6FigureJobs is unique for its focus on only employment opportunities that pay over $100,000 per annum.

Contact Information

Name: Anne Hunt Cheevers
Phone: 800-605-5154 x301

E-Mail: anne.cheevers@6figurejobs.com

SnagAJob.com

www.snagajob.com
SnagAJob.com, Inc.

GENERAL SITE INFORMATION

Date activated online:	2000
Location of site headquarters:	Glen Allen, VA
Number of people who visit the site:	6,000,000 unique visitors/month
Time spent on site:	6:40 minutes/visit

JOB POSTINGS

Post full time jobs:	Yes
Post part time/contract/consulting jobs:	Yes - Part time
Most prevalent types of jobs posted:	SM, Food Service, Retail
Distribution:	National - USA
Number of job postings:	200,000+
Top salary levels of jobs:	Hourly
Source of postings:	Employers, Staffing

RESUME SERVICES

Are resumes or profiles posted on the site:	Yes
How long can you store:	Indefinitely
Who can post a resume:	Those registered
Fee to post:	None
Confidentiality available:	Yes

OTHER SERVICES

Is a listserv or discussion forum offered:	Yes
Are assessment instruments offered:	Yes
Automated job agent:	Yes
Career info provided:	Yes
Links to other sites:	Yes

SITE'S SELF DESCRIPTION

SnagAJob.com, the nation's largest job search site and online community, has helped connect hourly workers with quality full-time and part-time jobs in a wide range of industries since 2000. Headquartered in Richmond, VA, SnagAJob.com also provides both job seekers and employers with valued insights and a cutting-edge interface that are unique to hourly employment.

Contact Information

Name: Customer Service
Phone: 804-236-9934   E-Mail: info@snagajob.com

SPIE Career Center

www.spie.org/careercenter

SPIE - The International Society for Optics and Photonics

GENERAL SITE INFORMATION

Date activated online:	2001
Location of site headquarters:	Bellingham, WA
Number of people who visit the site:	6,500 unique visitors/month
Time spent on site:	3:30 minutes/visit

JOB POSTINGS

Post full time jobs:	Yes
Post part time/contract/consulting jobs:	Yes - All
Most prevalent types of jobs posted:	EN
Distribution:	International
Number of job postings:	660
Top salary levels of jobs:	$101-150K, $151-200K/yr
Source of postings:	Employers, Staffing

RESUME SERVICES

Are resumes or profiles posted on the site:	Yes
How long can you store:	1 year
Who can post a resume:	Those in the field
Fee to post:	None
Confidentiality available:	Yes

OTHER SERVICES

Is a listserv or discussion forum offered:	No
Are assessment instruments offered:	No
Automated job agent:	Yes
Career info provided:	Yes
Links to other sites:	Yes

SITE'S SELF DESCRIPTION

Your source for optics and photonics jobs and talent. Recruit your next hire or find your next job on the SPIE Career Center. Job seekers can search job listings, set up email alerts, and view the 'Advice+Tools' section. Employers may post jobs and gain access to a resume database, create a Resume Alert, and participate in job fairs held at SPIE conferences.

Contact Information

Name: Sara Leibert

Phone: 360-715-3705   E-Mail: jobsales@spie.org

TalentZoo.com

www.talentzoo.com
TalentZoo, Inc.

GENERAL SITE INFORMATION

Date activated online:	2001
Location of site headquarters:	Atlanta, GA
Number of people who visit the site:	250,000 unique visitors/month
Time spent on site:	5:40 minutes/visit

JOB POSTINGS

Post full time jobs:	Yes
Post part time/contract/consulting jobs:	Yes - All
Most prevalent types of jobs posted:	Advertising, New Media, Creative
Distribution:	National - USA
Number of job postings:	500
Top salary levels of jobs:	Up to $200K/yr
Source of postings:	Employers, Staffing

RESUME SERVICES

Are resumes or profiles posted on the site:	Yes
How long can you store:	Indefinitely
Who can post a resume:	Those registered
Fee to post:	None
Confidentiality available:	Yes

OTHER SERVICES

Is a listserv or discussion forum offered:	No
Are assessment instruments offered:	No
Automated job agent:	Yes
Career info provided:	Yes
Links to other sites:	No

SITE'S SELF DESCRIPTION

TalentZoo.com is a nationwide career site focused on the communications industry. We offer a job board, resume access, news and trends and unique content authored by industry leaders for our users. The site was named by Forbes as "Best of the Web."

Contact Information

Name: Amy Hoover
Phone: 404-607-1955   E-Mail: support@talentzoo.com

TopUSAJobs.com

www.topusajobs.com
TopUSAJobs.com, Inc.

GENERAL SITE INFORMATION

Date activated online:	2003
Location of site headquarters:	North Miami Beach, FL
Number of people who visit the site:	4,000,000+ unique visitors/month
Time spent on site:	5.0 page views/visitor

JOB POSTINGS

Post full time jobs:	Yes
Post part time/contract/consulting jobs:	Yes - All
Most prevalent types of jobs posted:	Wide variety
Distribution:	National - USA
Number of job postings:	1,500,000+
Top salary levels of jobs:	Hourly to $250K+/yr
Source of postings:	Employers, Staffing

RESUME SERVICES

Are resumes or profiles posted on the site:	No
How long can you store:	N/A
Who can post a resume:	N/A
Fee to post:	N/A
Confidentiality available:	N/A

OTHER SERVICES

Is a listserv or discussion forum offered:	No
Are assessment instruments offered:	No
Automated job agent:	No
Career info provided:	Yes
Links to other sites:	Yes

SITE'S SELF DESCRIPTION

TopUSAJobs.com, the first pay-per-click job search engine, is a leading provider of targeted candidate traffic to hundreds of job boards, companies and staffing agencies. Since 2003, TopUSAJobs has given job seekers free access to millions of jobs nationwide with our easy-to-use search functionalities.

Contact Information

Name: Shelly Mudd
Phone: 866-712-5627   E-Mail: shelly@topusajobs.com

VetJobs

www.vetjobs.com
VetJobs.com, Inc.

GENERAL SITE INFORMATION

Date activated online:	November, 1999
Location of site headquarters:	Roswell, GA
Number of people who visit the site:	110,000 unique visitors/month
Time spent on site:	21.0 page views/visitor

JOB POSTINGS

Post full time jobs:	Yes
Post part time/contract/consulting jobs:	Yes - All
Most prevalent types of jobs posted:	AD, EN, IS, MG, OP, Defense
Distribution:	International
Number of job postings:	37,000
Top salary levels of jobs:	$75-100K, $201-250K/yr
Source of postings:	Employers, Staffing

RESUME SERVICES

Are resumes or profiles posted on the site:	Yes
How long can you store:	Indefinitely
Who can post a resume:	Those in the field
Fee to post:	None
Confidentiality available:	Yes

OTHER SERVICES

Is a listserv or discussion forum offered:	No
Are assessment instruments offered:	Yes
Automated job agent:	No
Career info provided:	Yes
Links to other sites:	Yes

SITE'S SELF DESCRIPTION

Veterans of Foreign Wars sponsored VetJobs is the leading military-related job board on the Internet. The jobs database is available to anyone who visits the site, but to post a resume a candidate must have been associated with the military family. Thousands of veterans worldwide have found jobs with the hundreds of employers who use VetJobs to reach the veteran market.

Contact Information

Name: Ted Daywalt
Phone: 770-993-5117   E-Mail: tdaywalt@vetjobs.com

WallStJobs.com
www.wallstjobs.com
WallStJobs.com, Inc.

GENERAL SITE INFORMATION

Date activated online:	1999
Location of site headquarters:	Garden City, NY
Number of people who visit the site:	64,238 unique visitors/month
Time spent on site:	12:40 minutes/visit

JOB POSTINGS

Post full time jobs:	Yes
Post part time/contract/consulting jobs:	Yes - All
Most prevalent types of jobs posted:	FA, MG, OP, SM
Distribution:	National - USA
Number of job postings:	1,565
Top salary levels of jobs:	$76-100K, 101-150K/yr
Source of postings:	Employers

RESUME SERVICES

Are resumes or profiles posted on the site:	Yes
How long can you store:	Indefinitely
Who can post a resume:	Those in the field
Fee to post:	None
Confidentiality available:	Yes

OTHER SERVICES

Is a listserv or discussion forum offered:	No
Are assessment instruments offered:	No
Automated job agent:	Yes
Career info provided:	Yes
Links to other sites:	Yes

SITE'S SELF DESCRIPTION

Launched in 1999, WallStJobs.com has become one of the most well-recognized and well-respected recruitment resources for the financial services industry. We know the industry because we are staffed by financial services professionals as well as recruiters with prior experience at personnel agencies serving the financial services community.

Contact Information

Name: Robert Graber
Phone: 516-873-8100   E-Mail: rgraber@wallstjobs.com

Work In Sports
www.workinsports.com
Work In Sports, LLC

GENERAL SITE INFORMATION

Date activated online:	2000
Location of site headquarters:	Scottsdale, AZ
Number of people who visit the site:	250,000 unique visitors/month
Time spent on site:	3:00 minutes/visit

JOB POSTINGS

Post full time jobs:	Yes
Post part time/contract/consulting jobs:	Yes - Part time
Most prevalent types of jobs posted:	MG, SM, Customer Service, Sports-related
Distribution:	National - USA
Number of job postings:	3,100
Top salary levels of jobs:	$76-100K, $101-150K/yr
Source of postings:	Employers, Other sites

RESUME SERVICES

Are resumes or profiles posted on the site:	Yes
How long can you store:	Indefinitely
Who can post a resume:	Those registered
Fee to post:	None
Confidentiality available:	Yes

OTHER SERVICES

Is a listserv or discussion forum offered:	No
Are assessment instruments offered:	No
Automated job agent:	Yes
Career info provided:	Yes
Links to other sites:	Yes

SITE'S SELF DESCRIPTION

Work In Sports is the complete sports employment resource, working with pro teams, leagues, facilities, NCAA athletic departments and other organizations in the sports industry. Employers can post unlimited jobs and internships and search the resume database of qualified applicants at no charge.

Contact Information

Name: John Mellor
Phone: 480-905-8077   E-Mail: jmellor@workinsports.com

Workopolis
www.workopolis.com
Toronto Star Newspapers, Ltd. and Square Victoria Digital Properties Inc.

GENERAL SITE INFORMATION

Date activated online:	2000
Location of site headquarters:	Toronto, Ontario, Canada
Number of people who visit the site:	1,600,000 unique visitors/month
Time spent on site:	6:30 minutes/visit

JOB POSTINGS

Post full time jobs:	Yes
Post part time/contract/consulting jobs:	Yes - All
Most prevalent types of jobs posted:	IS, SM, Health, Trades
Distribution:	National - Canada
Number of job postings:	30,000+
Top salary levels of jobs:	Not Reported
Source of postings:	Employers, Staffing

RESUME SERVICES

Are resumes or profiles posted on the site:	Yes
How long can you store:	Indefinitely
Who can post a resume:	Those registered
Fee to post:	None
Confidentiality available:	Yes

OTHER SERVICES

Is a listserv or discussion forum offered:	No
Are assessment instruments offered:	Yes
Automated job agent:	Yes
Career info provided:	Yes
Links to other sites:	Yes

SITE'S SELF DESCRIPTION

Workopolis.com is the Canadian leader in the Internet recruitment and career transition solutions field, helping employers and candidates connect with each other online. Along with offering employers the tools to post jobs online and search a database of millions of candidate resumes, Workopolis also offers ground-breaking employer branding tools.

Contact Information

Name: Jason Karsh
Phone: 416 957-8385   E-Mail: support@workopolis.com

WorkplaceDiversity.com
www.workplacediversity.com
WorkplaceDiversity.com, LLC

GENERAL SITE INFORMATION

Date activated online:	1999
Location of site headquarters:	Livingston, NJ
Number of people who visit the site:	153,000 unique visitors/month
Time spent on site:	8.5 page views/visitor

JOB POSTINGS

Post full time jobs:	Yes
Post part time/contract/consulting jobs:	Yes - All
Most prevalent types of jobs posted:	Professional
Distribution:	National - USA
Number of job postings:	9,000
Top salary levels of jobs:	$101-150K, $151-200K/yr
Source of postings:	Employers

RESUME SERVICES

Are resumes or profiles posted on the site:	Yes
How long can you store:	Indefinitely
Who can post a resume:	Anyone
Fee to post:	None
Confidentiality available:	Yes

OTHER SERVICES

Is a listserv or discussion forum offered:	No
Are assessment instruments offered:	Yes
Automated job agent:	Yes
Career info provided:	Yes
Links to other sites:	Yes

SITE'S SELF DESCRIPTION

WorkplaceDiversity.com, the source for diversity talent®, is the preeminent job search Web-site for corporate recruiters who are seeking experienced diverse talent. Our goal is to create a connection between companies that support diversity and experienced, distinct candidates by providing one location for recruiters to post open positions.

Contact Information

Name: Mike Monsport
Phone: 972-992-7311   E-Mail: sales@workplacediversity.com

About The Editor

Peter Weddle has been the CEO of three HR consulting companies, a Partner in the Hay Group and the recipient of a Federal award for leadership-related research. Described by *The Washington Post* as "… a man filled with ingenious ideas," he has authored or edited over two dozen books and been a columnist for *The Wall Street Journal, National Business Employment Weekly* and CNN. com.

Peter is now the CEO of WEDDLE's Research & Publications, a company which specializes in employment and workforce issues. WEDDLE's Guides to Internet employment sites are the gold standard of their genre, leading the American Staffing Association to call Weddle the "Zagat of the online employment industry." He also currently serves as the CEO of the International Association of Employment Web Sites, the trade organization for the global online employment services industry.

His most recent books, *The Career Activist Republic* and *Work Strong: Your Personal Career Fitness System,* offer a frank yet positive assessment of the challenges and opportunities available to working men and women in 21st Century America. His forthcoming novel, *Walden 4G: A Novel About Rediscovering Hopefulness (and America's Secret Utopia),* is due out in early 2012.

Weddle is a graduate of the United States Military Academy at West Point. He has attended Oxford University and holds advanced degrees from Middlebury College and Harvard University.

Don't miss any of Peter Weddle's thought-provoking and inspiring books.

Get them at Amazon.com or at Weddles.com today.